DEVELOPING
LIFE~CHANGING
BIBLE STUDY CURRICULUM

BY PHYLLIS BENNETT

DEVELOPING LIFE-CHANGING BIBLE STUDY CURRICULUM
TABLE OF CONTENTS

GOAL #1: DEVELOPING BIBLE STUDY CURRICULUM

SECTION A: INDUCTIVE BIBLE STUDY SKILLS

COURSE GOAL #1:

This course provides the opportunity for students to:
Learn how to **develop Bible study curriculum** for women, men and coed groups that is biblically sound, relevant, and applicable to all arenas of an individual's life.

ACCORDING TO SCRIPTURE, WHY ARE SMALL GROUPS NECESSARY FOR MINISTRY TO PEOPLE?

I. The Counsel of Jethro: Exodus 18:13-27

A. Why was Moses' leadership ineffective?

B. What was Jethro's assessment of Moses' leadership?

C. What was Jethro's counsel to make Moses and the people more effective?

II. The Modeling of Jesus: Mark 3:13-18

A. What do you learn about community (size, nature, function) from the modeling of Jesus?

B. What relationships exist between the Great Commission, "Disciple all Nations," (Matthew 28:19) and Jesus' selection of the Twelve?

III. The Early Church:

The small group was the basic unit of the church's life during its first two centuries. There were no church buildings, and Christians met in private homes. The entertaining room in a moderately well-to-do house could hold comfortably about 30 people. Record all you can about the early "house church."

A. Acts 2:42-47

Pages 7-13 Adapted from Tom Erickson's Leadership Training Manual

B. Acts 5:42

C. Romans 16:3-5

D. 1 Corinthians 16:19

E. Colossians 4:15

IV. The "One Anothers"

Throughout Scripture a certain quality of fellowship is described that simply cannot be accomplished apart from a small group. Record what is commanded, check where you are in your present experience, and consider how a small group is uniquely conducive to its fulfillment. These relationships do not have to happen in a small group, but they do have to happen. If you are not experiencing these kinds of relationships, the right kind of group will make a significant contribution to your growth.

SCRIPTURE	THE RELATIONSHIP	MY PRESENT EXPERIENCE
James 5:16	I confess my faults to others	
1 Peter 1:22		
Hebrews 10:24		
Galatians 6:2		
Colossians 3:16		
1 Peter 4:9, 10		
Romans 15:14		
Romans 12:10		
Ephesians 4:32		

ACCORDING TO HISTORY AND THEOLOGY, WHY ARE SMALL GROUPS NECESSARY FOR MINISTRY TO PEOPLE?

History

"Virtually every major movement of spiritual renewal in the Christian Church has been accompanied by a return to the small group and the proliferation of such groups in private homes for Bible study, prayer, and discussion of the faith."

Howard Synder, The Problem of Wineskins (page 164)

The lesson of history is that small groups are often the source of large results in the church and society. When God's people gather to pray, study, and fellowship with each other, amazing things can happen. Some significant small group movements include:

- θ The "Collegia Pietatis" of Philip Jacob Spener
- θ The "Bands and Choirs" of Count Zinzendorf
- θ The "Class Meetings" of John Wesley
- θ The "Home Cells" of Dr. Paul Yonggi Cho

Theology

"So God created man in his own image, in the image of God he created him: male and female He created them." Genesis 1:27

The triune God who lives eternally as a fellowship of persons created us in his image - as male and female who are to live in open reciprocal fellowship with each other (Genesis 1:27-28). In the first creation account, humanity was created (Genesis 1). In the second account (Genesis 2:15-25), individuals (Adam and Eve) were created one after the other.

Theologically, the "we precedes the I." The image of God is constituted as community or co-humanity. Therefore, small group-ness is a "way of life," and not just another program.

God, who exists as community, builds life in the context of community. Church, Bible study, leadership, counseling, family development, and healing should be community experiences. Individualism and isolationism are movements away from community, which is the essence of God. God models for us and calls us to community and to family.

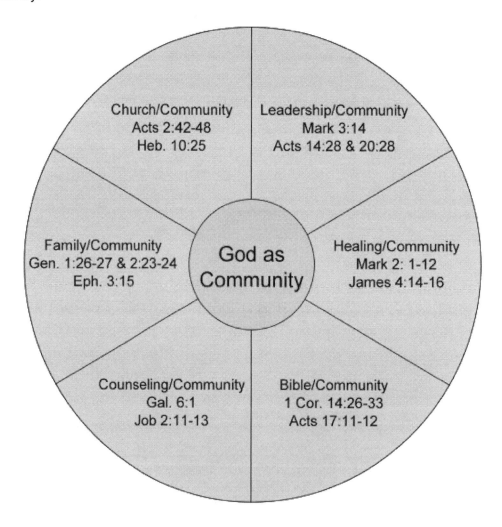

How do each of the above verses demonstrate God's heart for community?

WHEN YOUR SMALL GROUP MEETS, WHY STUDY THE BIBLE?

Why is the Bible so important?

I. It answers life's BIG questions.

From the time a child enters the universe, questions about life and integration with the world float in the mind.

- Why do I exist? Better yet, why does the universe exist? How do I fit into it? Is everything here by chance? Where does life come from?
- How can I know what is right and wrong? Are there any standards by which to evaluate behavior? Is there good and evil? Who determines this?
- How can I know anything for sure? Does what I perceive correspond to reality? How do I know that I am not out of synch with what is there? Can I trust myself?

> *"The God who is Trinity has spoken and He is not silent. There is no use having a silent God. We would not know anything about Him. He has spoken and told us what He is and that He existed before all else, and so we have the answer to the existence of what is."*
> *Francis A. Schaeffer*
> "He is There and He is Not Silent"

All religions and philosophies have been founded to answer these. The Bible gives the most reasonable explanation for everything that exists and for the meaning of life. The Bible presents an infinite-personal God as the answer to the big questions of life.

II. It provides guidance for daily life.

Rather than a dusty book of history, the Bible is as relevant to life as CNN or today's newspaper. More than that, it enables us to "participate in God's nature and escape the corruption in the world caused by evil desires" (2 Peter 1:4).

> *"His divine power has given us everything we need for life and godliness through our knowledge of Him who called us by his own glory and goodness."*
> *2 Peter 1:3*

Where God's Word is heard and obeyed, there is life, joy, peace, love, hope, gentleness, wisdom, maturity, forgiveness, and patience. Where God's Word is strongly present, there is a minimum of broken lives, divorce, child abuse, pain, racism, prejudice, immorality, lying, cheating, and quarreling. Knowing God's Word gives life meaning in the daily grind.

WHAT GOALS SHOULD I HAVE FOR PERSONAL BIBLE STUDY?

Studying the Bible is one of the worthiest things any of us can ever do. However, we need to study it for the right reasons and in the way that is most effective. In order to know the goals of personal Bible study we need to ask two much broader questions –

what does God expect of me and why am I here?

One of the great works of the faith, the Westminster Shorter Catechism, summarizes scriptural teaching in a series of questions and answers. The first asks, "What is the chief end of man?" and responds with, "The chief end of man is to glorify God and enjoy Him forever."

When Jesus was asked, in Matthew 22:36-40, "Teacher, which is the greatest commandment in the Law?" he replied, "'Love the Lord your God with all your heart and with all your soul and with all your mind.' This is the first and greatest commandment. And the second is like it: 'Love your neighbor as yourself.' All the Law and the Prophets hang on these two commandments."

These verses make it clear that our personal Bible study should not be a pointless wandering through the Word. Instead, it should focus on helping us glorify and enjoy God by learning how to love Him and our neighbors.

In brief, the goal of our personal Bible study should be the transformation of our lives into ones that please the Father and serve others.

I. Proper goals for personal Bible study
    A. Better understand God
        1. Who He is
        2. What He cares about
        3. Why He cares about us
        4. The history of His dealing with His people
        5. His plan for the future of His people
    B. Know God's will for my life
        1. Morally – how ought we to live in this world of ours?
        2. Specifically – what does the Father expect of me?
    C. Have my life changed into what God wants it to be
        1. Apply what I learn about Him and His will for me
        2. Have that application turn into visible results

> "Be diligent to present yourself approved to God, a worker who does not need to be ashamed, rightly handling the word of truth."
> 1 Timothy 2:15

II. Improper goals for personal Bible study
    A. Self satisfaction
    B. Winning the "I know more than you do" contests
    C. Impressing others

In other words, studying the Bible is about God, who He is, how He works in our world and our lives, what He expects of us, how we are to serve and worship Him, etc. One should not study scripture for self-serving reasons.

TO STUDY SCRIPTURE, WHAT APPROACH SHOULD I TAKE?

There are many ways to study scripture, each with its own strengths and weaknesses. In this leadership course we will be teaching the Inductive Method of Bible study.

A. Deductive Bible Study
1. Begin with principle, theological viewpoint or premise, usually taken from texts outside the Bible, from other teachers or from personal insights.
2. Based on making statements and proving them or backing them up with Scripture.
3. **Result: God speaks to others who speak to you.**

B. Inductive Bible Study
1. Begin with biblical text being studied.
2. Uses Bible as primary text.
3. Based on asking questions of the text and letting the text speak for itself.
4. Technical term is exegesis—"drawing out" the meaning of the text.
5. **Result: God speaks to YOU!**

A. The process of learning
1. True learning comes from involvement.
2. Involvement is directly related to the degree to which we raise questions.
3. Questions are the bridge from observations to accurate interpretation.

B. How we hold on to what we learn
1. We retain 10%% of what we read, 20% of what we see..
2. We retain 20% of what we hear.
3. We retain 50% of what we see and hear.
4. We retain 80% of what we do.
3. Writing down our questions helps us organize our data.
4. It also challenges us to use many different kinds of questions.

The process of Inductive Bible Study gets us involved by challenging us to ask questions and develop observations. It reinforces learning by helping us develop the habit of writing down key results from our study.

13

WHAT ARE THE BASIC STEPS OF INDUCTIVE BIBLE STUDY?

There are many approaches to personal Bible study. The Inductive Bible Study Method we will be using is an orderly, structured approach to understanding and applying scripture. It has four steps:

1. **OBSERVATION** – draw out what the text says
2. **INTERPRETATION** – determine what it means
3. **CORRELATION** – define how the text is connected with the rest of scripture, culture, or my life
4. **APPLICATION** – specify what the text means to me and how it should affect my life in real and specific ways

> *Exegesis - to draw out the meaning of the text*

> You are about to be introduced to several different inductive study tools needed for each of the above steps in the inductive process. Not every skill needs to be completed on every passage. Not every tool in your tool kit is needed every time. Consider them as available tools in a toolbox, helpful Bible study tools you may want to use to aid you in discovering an accurate interpretation of the text.

I. OBSERVATION — WHAT THE TEXT SAYS

The purpose of this phase of the inductive study process is to develop a strong sense of the text, to know what it says and be able to explain it to someone else. This phase is the basis for each succeeding one.

OBSERVATION IS THE ART OF SEEING WHAT IS THERE AND ITS SIGNIFICANT. WHAT SHOULD YOU OBSERVE?

> **I have six faithful serving men who taught me all I know. Their names are what and where and when and how and why and who.**
> **Rudyard Kipling .**

1. **LOOK FOR 5 W's and 1 H**
   - **WHO** wrote it? received it? spoke it? are the main characters and their characteristics?

   - **WHAT** is the main topic? main problem being addressed? are the main events? the event details? the major ideas? are the characters doing? discipline, correction or commendation is being provided?

   - **WHERE** was it written? said? take place? can it be found on a map?

- **WHEN** was it written? said? take place? will it happen?

  Mark all references to time with a time symbol: 🕐

Now	When
Then	Until
After	Immediately

- **HOW** will it happen? it is done? do the main characters interact? did the passage end? is the outcome shaped?

- **WHY** was it written? was the action taken? (Caution: Only ask why if the text tells you why - otherwise you will be speculating and not truly observing the meaning of the text.)

2. LOOK FOR KEY WORDS, especially ones that repeat, such as . . .

God	Riches	Jesus Christ	Heaven
Holy Spirit	Grace	Church	Devil

1. Key words are words that are either repeated or seem important to the understanding of the text.
2. Use symbols and/or various colors to mark them.
3. Make a list for each key word in the margins and draw conclusions.

3. LOOK FOR CONTRASTS

Contrasts are two ideas or concepts that stand in opposition to each other. Consider the contrast between the following two verses:
- θ Ephesians 2:1 you were dead in your transgressions
- θ Ephesians 2:4 but God...made us alive with Christ

Words to look for:

But	However
Yet	Although

Mark all contrasts with: $\neq$

4. LOOK FOR COMPARISONS

Comparisons are where the text points out similarities or differences between ideas, concepts, conditions, etc.

Words to look for:

Like	Also	Likewise
As	So	The same as
Just as	And	

Mark all comparisons with: ≈

5. & 6. LOOK FOR CONCLUSIONS AND/OR CAUSE AND EFFECT

Conclusions are summary statements; a central point
Cause and effect highlights what caused a situation and what
resulted from it:

Words to look for:

Wherefore	Therefore	Finally
For this reason	Then	So then
So that	Consequently	If, If then

Mark all conclusions or cause and effect with:

7. LOOK FOR GENERAL TO PARTICULAR (or vice versa)

General to particular implies movement in thought from the general or big
picture to the more specific and detailed. No specific "words to look for."
Example of general to particular: Galatians 5:19 "The acts of the sinful
nature are obvious—sexual immorality, etc.
Example of particular to general: Hebrews 11 gives examples of people of
faith and then concludes by saying, "Men of whom the world is not worthy."

8. LOOK FOR PROGRESSION

Progression means that a theme is amplified by additional thoughts,
insights, descriptions or clarifications. Each step of the progression builds
on the one before. The progression often moves to a conclusion. No
specific "words to look for." Example: 2 Peter 1:5 "Add to your faith,
goodness, to goodness knowledge,. . . "

9. LOOK FOR LISTS

SIMPLE LIST - A simple list is found in the passage itself and can be
numbered in the text. Example: Romans 8:35-36 lists that which cannot
separate us from the love of Christ. 1 Timothy 3:2-7 lists the qualifications
of an elder.

TOPICAL LIST A topical list is a comprehensive list of all the words or
phrases that relate to one particular theme or topic in a passage.
Examples: Luke 15—lists lost items
John 10—lists descriptions of the Good Shepherd.

CREATE A TITLE FOR EACH PARAGRAPH, CHAPTER AND BOOK
1. Review key word lists, contrasts, comparisons, and conclusions

2. Decide on a summary statement of your own choosing

3. Use a phrase and be concise (2-4 words)

NOW IT'S YOUR TURN: Apply the above principles of observation to the following verses. Remember that all ten principles may not apply to every passage.

Observation Practice
Philippians 4:6-7

"Do not be anxious about anything, but in everything, by prayer and petition with thanksgiving, present your requests to God. 7 And the peace of God, which transcends all understanding will guard your hearts and minds in Christ Jesus.

Your Observations: What Do You See?

1. 5 W's and H

2. Key or repeated words

3. Contrasts

4. Comparisons

5. Conclusions

6. Cause and Effect

7. General to Particular or Vice Versa

8. Progression

9 Lists

10. Title for Paragraph

What did you learn about the process of Bible study from completing this exercise?

II. INTERPRETATION — WHAT THE TEXT MEANS

In this second phase of Inductive Bible Study try to answer the question "What does the text mean?" Interpretation is understanding what the **author** meant without adding your own ideas or insights so as to avoid the sad but true cliché "everyone has their own interpretation of the Bible." In actuality, there is only one true interpretation of a text—the interpretation the author intended for his reading audience.

INTERPRETATION IS THE ART OF UNDERSTANDING THE AUTHOR'S INTENDED MEANING OF THE TEXT. HELPFUL HINTS FOR ACCURATE INTERPRETATION INCLUDE:

1. **ASK FOR THE HELP OF THE HOLY SPIRIT.**

2. **CONSIDER THE SETTING**
   a. Context of the passage
   b. Literary form of the passage
   c. Historical Setting
   d. Cultural Context

3. **CONSIDER THE CONTEXT RULE: Context rules in interpretation.**
   Most, if not all, false interpretations of scripture come because a passage is taken out of context.
   Consider the passage in light of what comes *before and after* the passage you are studying.
   Think or imagine yourself back in the culture, society and time period in which the passage was written.

4. **DETERMINE THE AUTHOR'S INTENDED MEANING FOR HIS OWN HEARERS BEFORE CONSIDERING THE MEANING FOR US TODAY.**

5. **INTERPRET WORDS IN THE USUAL LITERAL SENSE** unless you have reason to believe they are allegorical or figurative. Interpret figures of speech in the same way we use them in normal speech.

6. **STUDY WORD MEANINGS**
   For key words, repeated words or any words you cannot define, clearly locate the meaning of the word in a regular dictionary or Bible dictionary.
   a. Find same word in same book.
   b. Find same word by same author.
   c. Find same word in same testament. Find same word in other testament
      (Septuagint – Greek for the OT)

7. **STUDY GRAMMAR.** ie. verb tenses, singular and plural pronouns, etc.

8. **CROSS REFERENCE KEY WORDS OR PHASES.** Look up other scriptures that support, clarify or further explain the Bible passage. Scripture is the best interpreter of scripture. Draw relationships between texts. See how one passage helps explain another.
   Remember context. It is critical. A verse taken out of context and "engineered" to support an argument is not God's truth.
   Use a **concordance** to look up several references. A concordance might be found at the back of your Bible; it is a listing of words with reference to the places they are used in the Bible.

9. **INTERPRET HISTORICAL PASSAGES IN THE LIGHT OF TEACHING PASSAGES.** What did happen may or may not be what should have happened. What happened for one may or may not be for all.

10. **INTERPRET THE OLD TESTAMENT IN LIGHT OF THE NEW, AND THE NEW IN LIGHT OF THE OLD, KEEPING IN MIND GOD'S PROGRESSIVE REVELATION.**

11. **INTERPRET THE UNCLEAR PASSAGES IN THE LIGHT OF THE CLEAR PASSAGES.** (Whatever this unclear passage means we know it doesn't mean because . . .)

12. **CHURCH HISTORY IS IMPORTANT, BUT IT DOES NOT HAVE THE FINAL WORD. THE WORD OF GOD IS OUR FINAL AUTHORITY FOR FAITH AND PRACTICE.**

13. **CONSIDER FUNDAMENTAL QUESTIONS ASKED OF EVERY PASSAGE:**
    - Why did God write this passage and put it in His book?
    - What are the **permanent principles** or **timeless truths** in this passage?
    - What does this passage say about **God, Jesus**, the **Holy Spirit**?
    - What does this passage say about **mankind**?
    - What does this passage say about **sin** and **evil**?
    - What does this passage say about **right** or **wrong attitudes**?
    - What does this passage say about **good** or **bad examples?**
    - What does this passage say about **truth** or **error?**

14. **LOOK FOR THE CENTRAL TRUTH, THE MAIN THEME OR THE MAIN POINT OF THE PASSAGE,** while understanding that the passage will have secondary or complementary points to the main point of the passage. Look for the complementary points of the passage as well.

15. **MAKE A LIST OF QUESTIONS WITHOUT TRYING TO ANSWER THEM AT THIS TIME.** Write down anything that comes to mind that may eventually need an answer (see next page).

16. **ONLY AS A LAST RESORT, CHECK COMMENTARIES** (see pages 25 for help in wisely choosing and using commentaries).

Eight types of interpretive questions are given below. Use several questions of each type whenever possible

TYPE   **DESCRIPTION**
Meaning   What does this word or phrase mean?
Significance   What is the significance of this?
Relationship   How are these related to each other?
Identification Who is this or did this?
Temporal   When was, is, or will this be done?
Local   Where did this happen?
Implication   What does this imply? (also touches on applications)
Rational   Why is this here?

Example questions for Philippians 3:7: "But whatever was to my profit I now consider loss for the sake of Christ."

OBSERVATIONS	INTERPRETIVE QUESTIONS
"but" is a word of contrast	What is contrasted previously to verse 3?
with verses 3-6, "what things" points out specific areas of concern	What specific things is Paul concerned with?
"gain" signifies a previous perspective on things	What does the word gain mean? When were these considered a gain? In what way were they a gain? How can *gain* for Paul be *loss* for Christ?
"have counted" is past tense	What does the word count mean? When did Paul count these as loss? What is involved in counting something as a loss?

Interpretation Practice

NOW IT'S YOUR TURN:

From your observations made previously on Philippians 4:6-7 (place in left-hand column), ask interpretive questions as demonstrated on page 20 (principle 15).

Philippians 4:6-7

The text:

"6 Do not be anxious about anything, but in everything, by prayer and petition, with thanksgiving, present your requests to God. 7 And the peace of God, which transcends all understanding, will guard your hearts and your minds in Christ Jesus. "

OBSERVATIONS	INTERPRETIVE QUESTIONS

Interpretation Practice

NOW IT'S YOUR TURN: Apply the sixteen principles of interpretation to the following verses. Remember that all sixteen may not apply to every passage.

16 PRINCIPLES OF INTERPRETATION	
1. Ask for help from Holy Spirit 2. Consider the setting. 3. Consider the context rule. 4. Determine the author's intended meaning. 5. Interpret words in the usual literal sense. 6. Study word meanings. 7. Study grammar 8. Cross reference key words or phrases.	9. Interpret historical passages in light of teaching passages. 10. Interpret Old Testament in the light of the new. 11. Interpret the unclear passages in light of the clear. 12. Church history is important but it does not have the final word. 13. Consider fundamental questions asked of every passage. 14. Look for the central truth, theme or main point of the passage as well as the complementary points. 15. Make a list of questions without trying to answer them. 16. Only as a last resort, check commentaries.

Philippians 4:6-7

"6 Do not be anxious about anything, but in everything, by prayer and petition, with thanksgiving, present your requests to God. 7 And the peace of God, which transcends all understanding, will guard your hearts and your minds in Christ Jesus. "

Interpretative Insights:

1.

2.

3.

4.

5.

6.

7.

8.

9.

10.

THE HOW TO'S OF WORD STUDIES (PRINCIPLE #6)

What is a word study?

A word study is an attempt to define as accurately as possible the meaning of a biblical word in its context

Why is a word study important?

1. Words can have different meanings in different contexts
2. Meanings of words can change over time
3. Defining a word accurately can bring great clarity to a text

How do I choose a word for a word study?

1. Choose repeated words
2. Choose unclear words
3. Choose key verbs, nouns, or adjectives
4. Choose major theological concepts (covenant, righteousness, sin, etc.)
5. Choose words you feel may illuminate the entire passage

What steps do I take to complete a word study?

Step One:

Follow instructions given in your Bible software (Accordance for Macs, Logos for PC's. or Bible Study Tools.com (all 3 can be purchased on line)

OR

Blue letter Bible https://www.blueletterbible.org to access free on-line Bible software

OR

Locate the Strong's Concordance number of your word in one of the following resources:

The Complete Word Study New Testament by Spiros Zodhiates Th.D.
The Complete Word Study Old Testament by Spiros Zodhiates Th.D.
   (both come in King James and New American Standard versions)

Example of word study for the word "trial" in James 1:2
v. 2 My brethren, count it all joy when ye fall into divers "temptations" (3986) KJV
Note: Although Zhodiates is an English translation of the Bible into King James English, it is still possible to use its numbering system to determine the meaning of the word "trial" from the NIV or any other translation by determining its placement in the sentence (trial = temptation).

Step Two:

Use the Strong's number to locate the definition of "trial" in a *Strong's Exhaustive Concordance* KJV or NIV translation or in *The Englishman's Concordance.* Strong's gives all the definitions of the word *by number—3986* under one heading (in the back) and lists all the locations of the word *by name— temptation KJV or trial NIV* (in the front). The Englishman's Concordance lists every biblical location of the word *by number* with its varied definitions according to its location.

Step Three:

To complete **a thorough and accurate word study**, it is best **to list all the biblical locations of your word within the book you are studying (James).** List each of their definitions with their range of meanings. The Greek word for "trial" occurs twice within the book of James (James 1:2 and 1:12). However, the definition of this word is quite different within these two contexts:

James 1:2 *Strong's Concordance* would most precisely define it as *"a putting to proof by experiment of good, a discipline"*

James 1:12 *Strong's Concordance* would most precisely define this word as *"a putting to proof by experience of evil, temptation"*

Since Greek only has one word for both trial and temptation, it is ***important to choose its correct definition*** from Strong's as defined by its context.
The Englishman's Concordance **chooses for you** from the range of meanings a meaning that best fits the context. Strong's does not.

Step Four:

Whichever biblical tool you choose to use, it is still best to study first all the uses of the word in the book you are studying (step three) **and then in the testament (old or new) from which your word has been taken (step four).** Sometimes, but not always, this fourth step is necessary to make sure you are choosing an accurate definition.

Remember, CONTEXT always RULES in INTERPRETATION. Therefore the context will help you decide which definition is the best definition for your word from Strong's list of possible choices. Checking its meaning and context in other locations may greatly illuminate how the word is being used in the context of the verse you are studying.

Alternative Step Three and Four:

Vine's Complete Expository Dictionary of Old and New Testament Words is another excellent resource for definitions, although it defines a limited number of biblical words. It is arranged alphabetically by testament (i.e. "temptation"). After locating the Strong's number in *Zodiates*, find the word "temptation" with its varied meanings in *Vine's*. Since there are many English words that, when translated, may result in more than one Greek word, locating the correct Strong's number (3986) is imperative before using *Vine's*. Once you have located the correct number and word in *Vine's*, follow steps three and four above.

Why use *Vine's*? *Vine's* gives much more extensive definitions than *Strong's* or the *Englishman's Concordance* of the limited number of words it defines.

Interpretation Practice

NOW IT'S YOUR TURN: Complete a word study on the word peace from **Philippians 4:6-7 (principle 6).**

A WARNING ABOUT MISINTERPRETING SCRIPTURE—THE NEED TO CHECK COMMENTARIES FOR ACCURATE INTERPRETATION

Upon the completion of all biblical work, it is time to check commentaries to confirm or raise questions regarding your biblical insights. Commentaries will also give clarity regarding the literary form and the historical and grammatical accuracy of your biblical research. They can also be used to confirm or determine the author's original intent. Remember, you are to be looking for what the author intended for the passage to mean, not primarily what the passage meant to you. Below is an example of a poor interpretation of a passage that does not confirm the original author's intent. This inaccurate interpretation could have been eliminated if commentaries had been consulted. **Ramesh Richard, professor of Pastoral Ministries, World Missions, and International Studies at Dallas Theological Seminary,** says the following about interpretation:

Interpretation

The main criterion for a proper method of interpretation is that there be a demonstrable and reliable connection between the author's and the original audience's understanding of a given text and our interpretation. Really, the Bible can be made to say almost anything you may want it to say. The critical question is this: Are you saying what the Bible wanted to say? For example, I heard a fine message on Luke 19:29-40 offer the following truths:

Jesus and the Donkey

I. **You are like the donkey (vv. 29-30)**

    A. **You are tied to someone other than the owner to whom really belong (v. 30)**

    B. **You are still young—no one has sat on you (v. 30b)**

II. **Jesus commands you to be set free (v. 30c)**

    A. **He sets you free through his disciples (vv. 31-32)**

    B. **There will be objections when you are being freed to serve Christ (v. 33)**

    C. **But He has need of you (v. 34)**

III. **Are you Christ's donkey? (vv. 35-40)**

    A. **Is He riding on you?**

    B. **Are you bringing praise to Him?**

Can this sermon be preached? It already has been! Is it textually faithful? No! Why? Ask this critical question: Are these points what the author intended to convey and what the original audience understood through this narrative?

Dr. Richard evaluated this sermon as follows: Your preaching lacks textual authority. In the donkey story, from where in the text did the preacher get the authority to equate donkeys with human beings? Unless the sermon demonstrates that the biblical author intended the text to be used in this way, there will be no authority for it. Such interpretation lacks objective controls. The central proposition of your sermon is not discernibly related to or drawn from the central proposition of the text. The interpretation of the preacher (and therefore the force of the sermon) becomes arbitrary. The people will begin to see sermons at the preacher's whimsical use of a given text.

Proper methods of interpretation must form the backbone of the sermon. The preacher is first an exegete of Scripture before he is an expositor of Scripture.

Below are possible sources of commentaries and study helps. Many others can be found at well-stocked Christian bookstores.

RESOURCES

On-line

www.biblegateway.com (this has commentaries, dictionaries, etc. right on the website)

www.crosswalk.com (commentaries, dictionaries, concordances, encyclopedias etc. on the website)

www.biblenet.com (dictionaries, commentaries, chat rooms)

http://ivpress.gospelcom.net/cgi-ivpress/book.pl/code=1800 (commentaries)

www.Studylight.org (word studies in Hebrew and Greek)

www.studybibleforum.com (discussion board for questions/answers)

http://eword.gospelcom.net/comments/ (commentaries)

www.bible.org (study tools)

www.christiananswers.net (study tools)

BOOKS

(Available at Barnes and Noble, Borders, Tatnuck Books, http://www.christianbook.com/, www.amazon.com, and many other on-line bookstores.)

Bible Dictionaries (Vine's is the most readily available)

Bible Concordances (Strong's and Zondervan's are the most readily available)

Bible Encyclopedias and Overviews

Bible Commentaries (either for individual books of the Bible or collections of books)

Ramesh Richard, *Preparing Expository Sermons: A Seven-Step Method for Biblical Preaching* (Grand Rapids: Baker Books, 2001), 22-23.

III. CORRELATION — HOW THE TEXT CORRELATES WITH OTHER SCRIPTURES, CULTURE AND WITH MY LIFE PERSONALLY

No section of scripture exists in a vacuum. Rather, it connects to other sections of God's Word, the culture in which it was written, the culture of today, and our lives.

A. Scripture - list how this truth correlates with other scriptures
    1. Old Testament scriptures
    2. New Testament scriptures
    3. Biblical characters as examples (positive and negative)

B. Cultural – how does it correlate with various areas of culture?
    1. Economic
    2. Physical
    3. Political
    4. Recreational
    5. Social
    6. Sexual
    7. Ideological
    8. Psychological

C. Reflective – how does this truth relate to our relationships and past or present experiences?

    1. Spouse
    2. Children
    3. Friends
    4. Neighbors
    5. City
    6. Nation
    7. Workers
    8. World

Correlation Practice

NOW IT'S YOUR TURN: Correlate Philippians 4:6-7 with other parts of Scripture.

"6 Do not be anxious about anything, but in everything, by prayer and petition, with thanksgiving, present your requests to God. 7 And the peace of God, which transcends all understanding, will guard your hearts and your minds in Christ Jesus."

1.

2.

3.

4.

5.

The following two pages contain categories of contextualization for women's and

TODAY'S ISSUES FOR CONTEXTUALIZATION OF GOD'S WORD

Personal Interest

➢ **Mental Health**
- ✓ Depression
- ✓ Stress
- ✓ Making Choices
- ✓ Alcoholism
- ✓ Drug Addiction
- ✓ Emotional Problems
- ✓ Crisis issues

➢ **Physical Fitness**
- ✓ Diet and Nutrition
- ✓ Weight Control
- ✓ Exercise

➢ **Spiritual Growth and Renewal**
- ✓ Bible Study
- ✓ Prayer
- ✓ Time issues w/ busy schedules

Personal Relationships

➢ **Friendships**
- ✓ Being a friend
- ✓ Maintaining friendships
- ✓ Loneliness
- ✓ Estrangement in friendships
- ✓ Widowhood and friendships
- ✓ Singleness and Single-parenting and friendships

➢ **Children**
- ✓ Childbirth and preschool age
- ✓ Discipline
- ✓ Stepchildren
- ✓ Blended families
- ✓ Communication
- ✓ Teen morality and pregnancy
- ✓ Grandparents
- ✓ Working Mothers
- ✓ Job sharing to parent effectively

Personal Pain
- ✓ Suicide
- ✓ Pornography
- ✓ Divorce Recovery
- ✓ Widowhood
- ✓ Eating Disorders
- ✓ Domestic Violence
- ✓ Sexual Abuse
- ✓ Lesbianism
- ✓ Abortion Recovery
- ✓ Discontent in Singleness

➢ **Marriage**
- ✓ Marriage preservation
- ✓ Stages of a marriage
- ✓ Late Marriages/ older when having children
- ✓ Marital priority with children
- ✓ Parenting as a team
- ✓ Both partners working

➢ **Extended Family**
- ✓ In- laws
- ✓ Responsibility for parents
- ✓ Caring for the elderly
- ✓ Holiday related issues
- ✓ Grandmother Role

Personal Relationships Cont.
- ➢ **Divorce**
  - ✓ Avoiding divorce
  - ✓ Counseling
  - ✓ Financial/Legal aspects
  - ✓ Divorce Recovery
  - ✓ Single parenting
  - ✓ Remarriage

- ➢ **Workplace Relationships**
  - ✓ Teamwork in the Workplace
  - ✓ Co-ed Working Environments
  - ✓ Competition in Relationships
  - ✓ Evangelism in the Workplace
  - ✓ Friendships VS Working Relationships
  - ✓ Balance w/ home/ family/ church

Personal Goals
- ➢ **Self-improvement**
  - ✓ Personality and temperament
  - ✓ Self-image
  - ✓ Development and use of spiritual gifts
  - ✓ Childhood Related Issues
  - ✓ Art of Communication
  - ✓ Overcoming Boredom
  - ✓ Color, clothes, fashion
  - ✓ Physical Fitness
  - ✓ Personal Mission Statement
  - ✓ Goal Setting – 1, 5, 10 year goals

- ➢ **Suffering from Relationships**
  - ✓ Sickness and pain/ care for the care-giver
  - ✓ Death and dying
  - ✓ Tragedies to loved ones
  - ✓ Recovery and Rehabilitation
  - ✓ Rape, child-molesting, incest

- ➢ **Leadership and Job Advancement**
  - ✓ Education and training
  - ✓ Social Clubs
  - ✓ Political Involvement
  - ✓ Church Leadership

- ➢ **Organization**
  - ✓ Household
  - ✓ Personal
  - ✓ Home Decorating
  - ✓ Time Management

- ➢ **Stewardship**
  - ✓ God the owner, we the stewards
  - ✓ Overall Money Management
  - ✓ Giving – How and to What

Correlation Practice

NOW IT'S YOUR TURN: Correlate Philippians 4:6-7 with three men or women's issues.

"6 Do not be anxious about anything, but in everything, by prayer and petition, with thanksgiving, present your requests to God. 7 And the peace of God, which transcends all understanding, will guard your hearts and your minds in Christ Jesus."

1.

IV. APPLICATION —— WHAT THE TEXT MEANS TO ME

Application is responding to God's Word—in a personal, active dependent manner, trusting the Holy Spirit to bring about change in our lives.

The goal of Bible study, therefore, is the transformation of our lives into ones that please the Father as well as lives that empower us to serve others, changing not just *our* lives but the lives of those with whom we interact. In fact, one could define application as "the process of regulating everything we are, everything we think, and everything we do by the Word of God."

Here are some helpful insights about application from the pen of those who love God's Word. The first set (#1-5) come from Susan Rochin, a women's retreat speaker and Bible teacher from California.

#1... General Applications to Ask and Answer

What applications do you see...

- for the church today?
- for Christians in America?
- for men and women in your town or city, both Christ-followers and seekers?
- for those who think God is irrelevant to their lives?

> "The object of Bible study is changed lives. The Christian world is suffering from a deficiency of Vitamin A - Application. "
> Howard

#2... Now to the Nitty Gritty...

What does this passage say to **you** right now in **your** life? Ask **"So what?"** What is this supposed to mean to **me** right now? Think through your relationships, your immediate life circumstances, your emotions and attitudes, and the choices you need to make. Here is a list to get you started:

- **Relationships** (family, friends, neighbors, co-workers, fellow believers)
- **Conflicts** (marriage, children, extended family, work, neighborhood)
- **Personal Burdens** (sickness, death, loss of any kind, family pressures)
- **Difficult Situations** (stress, debt, hindrances, setbacks)
- **Character Weaknesses** (anger, fear, bitterness, lust, selfishness, integrity, image)
- **Lack of Resources** (time, energy, money, materials, information, talents, abilities)
- **Responsibilities** (work and family demands, home projects, church programs, volunteer efforts)
- **Opportunities** (learning, working, serving, moving, traveling)

#3... Apply the Main Point

Write out the **main point** of the passage. It is important to find and apply the **main point** of a passage; otherwise you might find yourself picking and choosing applications that are easy for you and unchallenging. Ask yourself the following:

- **As God is looking at my life today, how well does He think I'm applying this truth?**
- **What would this truth look like if applied to my life?**
- **How would my life be affected if I operated on the basis of this truth? What would change? What would remain the same?**
- What is already part of my thinking?
- What is new to me?
- What requires a change of thought? How can I make the change?
- What is already part of my action?
- What can be applied immediately to my behavior?
- What am I doing that is wrong?
- What action must I take immediately?
- What will I need to do at some future date?

#4... More Questions to Help with Application

- Is there a COMMAND to obey?
- Is there a PROMISE to claim?
- Is there a SIN to confess?
- Is there a WARNING to heed?
- Is there an EXAMPLE to follow?
- Is there an ERROR to avoid or correct?
- Is there an ACTION to take or avoid?
- Is there a HABIT to form or break?
- Is there a TRUTH to be believed?
- Is there an UNTRUTH to be discarded?
- Is there an ATTITUDE to change?
- Is there an ENCOURAGEMENT to speak?
- Is there a PRAYER to pray?
- Is there something to PRAISE?

#5... Pray your Application

Ask the Holy Spirit to help you apply the truth you've learned.
Use this passage and some of your cross-references for your daily quiet time.
Consider asking your class to pray for you in regard to your application. Your small group leader will help you write out your request.

#6... Some Dangers of Omitting Application

- You will accumulate facts without grasping their meaning for your life (Ecclesiastes 1:16-18).
- You will substitute emotional experiences for decisions of the will to believe and obey God (2 Corinthians 7:8-11).
- You will not become spiritually mature (Hebrews 5:13-14).
- You will become critical and proud (1 Corinthians 8:1).
- You will deceive yourself and miss the blessing (James 1:22-25).
- You will fall when the hard times come (Luke 6:46-49).

Application Practice

NOW IT'S YOUR TURN: Apply Philippians 4:6-7 using these 6 principles:

Principles of Application
1. General applications to ask: What applications do you see for the church? for Christians in America? your town? both Christ-followers and seekers? for those who think God is irrelevant?
2. Now to the nitty gritty: What does this passage say to you right now? relationships? conflicts? personal burdens? difficult situations? character weaknesses? lack of resources? responsibilities? opportunities?
3. Apply the main point: Is it a part of my thinking? do I need to change an attitude? a behavior?
4. More questions to ask: command to obey? promise to claim? sin to confess? warning to heed? example to follow? error to avoid? action to take? habit to form or break?truth to believe? prayer to pray?
5. Pray your application.
6. Dangers of omitting application.

"6 Do not be anxious about anything, but in everything, by prayer and petition, with thanksgiving, present your requests to God. 7 And the peace of God, which transcends all understanding, will guard your hearts and your minds in Christ Jesus."

1.

2.

3.

4.

5.

6.

#7... Some Warnings about Misapplying Scripture

From Tom Erickson, seminary professor and pastor:

The text applies to us in a similar manner as it applied to the early church. If we have been careful in our Bible study, interpretation will overcome our views regulated by traditions, prejudices, and brands of theology. God's Word to the early church is God's Word to us.

Some biblical texts are conditioned by first-century customs, local situations or Jewish or other ethnic traditions. Customs of the time regarding the wearing of hats, length of hair, drinking wine for stomach problems, a holy kiss, eating meat in a temple, silence of women in the church, women in the role of deacon, and styles of worship reflect the cultural attitudes of the first century and are not necessarily designed to be universally copied. It is important in application to distinguish between timeless teaching and principles as opposed to those that were linked to the time or culture.

From Haddon Robinson, a renown seminary professor and preacher:

"It's when we're applying Scripture that error is most likely to creep in . . .
What makes Bible application so prone to error? In application we attempt to take what we believe is the truth of the eternal God, which was given in a particular time and place and situation, and apply it to people in the modern world who live in another time, another place, and a very different situation. This is harder than it appears. The Bible is specific—Paul writes letters to particular churches; the stories are specific—but my audience is general."

Haddon Robinson's "Abstraction Ladder" is a wonderful aid in discerning how to apply the truth of Scripture starting from the biblical world. Some passages can be applied straight across into our modern world. Other texts require increasing abstraction in order to be applied. We climb the abstraction ladder by asking:
1) What does this text teach about God?
2) What does this text teach about human nature?

Some texts must be abstracted to their intent: e.g., "Don't boil a kid in its mother's milk means "Don't participate in idolatrous practices of the surrounding culture." Other texts go straight across, e.g., "Love your enemies."
Here is a picture of Robinson's Abstraction Ladder:

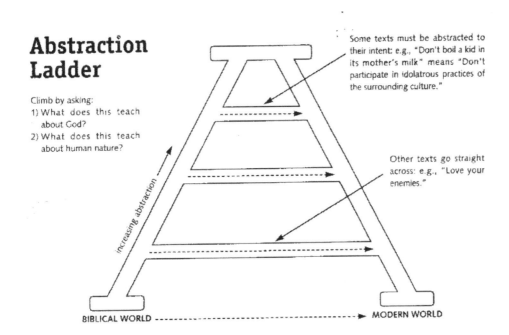

Application Practice

NOW IT'S YOUR TURN: Apply the abstraction ladder to a passage where you feel the abstraction ladder is needed:

BASIC ELEMENTS of the application phase of the inductive process:

A. MEDITATION

- Focus on parts of the text (whether a sentence, phrase, or a word) that you have interpreted and that speak to you.
- Turn it over in your mind until all sides of it have been examined.
- In the process, the implications of the text will become evident to you.

B. SUMMARY

Formulate simple truths that are meaningful to you.

Philippians 4:6 When presenting my request to God **with thanksgiving**, I am expressing my trust in God's capacity to provide a solution(s) to whatever is creating my anxiety.

Philippians 4:7 The peace of God will act like a referee, guarding my heart /mind from anxiety, whenever I choose to present my request to Him.

C. SELECTION

You may uncover many applications. Select some that will have the most impact, or are most needed, in your life.

- "I will thank God for His capacity to provide a solution for my child's struggles."
- "I will ask God for His peace to guard my heart and mind from anxiety when I think of relating to my boss."

The following chart may help you brainstorm methods for taking one application idea and applying it in several relational contexts. After brainstorming, select one relationship where you sense God nudging you to apply this idea to your personal life.

Phil.4:6-7 IDEA	RELATIONSHIPS	CONTEXTS	SELECT ONE APPLICATION
Displace worry with prayer	• Wife • Child • Church leaders • Boss	• Wife is sick • Depressed • Uncertain of church's direction • Expects too much	• I will pray each morning about my productivity on the job and wisdom in coping with my boss.

Application Practice

NOW IT'S YOUR TURN: Choose one idea from Philippians 4:6-7 and select one application of that to your life today.

OBSERVATION PRACTICE
TEACHING PASSAGE

1. Using the *Scripture Worksheet* of James 1 on the following pages, mark these key words: God (as well as synonyms for God), Jesus Christ (as well as synonyms for Jesus Christ), law, perseveres/perseverance, suffering/testing/endurance/trial, and tempt/evil/sin, and any other repeated words you can find In the margins, list everything you learn about these words.

2. What other words/and or phrases stand out to you in James 1? Mark these and list everything you learn about them in the margins.

3. Using the *Scripture Worksheet* for James 1 on the following pages, mark the observations listed below using symbols and/or colored pencils.

YOUR OBSERVATIONS? WHAT DO YOU SEE?
1. 5 W's and H 2. Time words. 3. Contrasts. 4. Comparisons 5. Conclusions 6. Cause and Effect 7. General to Particular (vice versa) 8. Progression 9. Lists 10. Title for paragraphs, for chapter

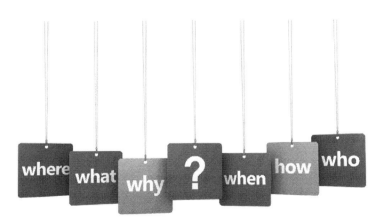

SCRIPTURE WORKSHEET TEACHING PASSAGE
James 1

1James, a servant of God and of the Lord Jesus Christ, to the twelve tribes scattered among the nations: Greetings.

2Consider it pure joy, my brothers, whenever you face trials of many kinds, 3because you know that the testing of your faith develops perseverance. 4Perseverance must finish its work so that you may be mature and complete, not lacking anything.

5If any of you lacks wisdom, he should ask God, who gives generously to all without finding fault, and it will be given to him. 6But when he asks, he must believe and not doubt, because he who doubts is like a wave of the sea, blown and tossed by the wind. 7That man should not think he will receive anything from the Lord; 8he is a double-minded man, unstable in all he does. 9The brother in humble circumstances ought to take pride in his high position. 10But the one who is rich should take pride in his low position, because he will pass away like a wild flower. 11For the sun rises with scorching heat and withers the plant; its blossom falls and its beauty is destroyed. In the same way, the rich man will fade away even while he goes about his business. 12Blessed is the man who perseveres under trial, because when he has stood the test, he will receive the crown of life that God has promised to those who love him. 13When tempted, no one should say, "God is tempting me." For God cannot be tempted by evil, nor does he tempt anyone; 14but each one is tempted when, by his own evil desire, he is dragged away and enticed. 15Then, after desire has conceived, it gives birth to sin; and sin, when it is full-grown, gives birth to death. 16Don't be deceived, my dear brothers. 17Every good and perfect gift is from above, coming down from the Father of the heavenly lights, who does not change like shifting shadows. 18He chose to give us birth through the word of truth, that we might be a

19My dear brothers, take note of this: Everyone should be quick to listen, slow to speak and slow to become angry,

20for man's anger does not bring about the righteous life that God desires.

21Therefore, get rid of all moral filth and the evil that is so prevalent and humbly accept the word planted in you, which can save you.

22Do not merely listen to the word, and so deceive yourselves. Do what it says.

23Anyone who listens to the word but does not do what it says is like a man who looks at his face in a mirror

24and, after looking at himself, goes away and immediately forgets what he looks like.

25But the man who looks intently into the perfect law that gives freedom, and continues to do this, not forgetting what he has heard, but doing it— he will be blessed in what he does.

26If anyone considers himself religious and yet does not keep a tight rein on his tongue, he deceives himself and his religion is worthless.

27Religion that God our Father accepts as pure and faultless is this: to look after orphans and widows in their distress and to keep oneself from being polluted by the world.

OBSERVATION PRACTICE
ALTERNATIVE TEACHING PASSAGE

1. Using the *Scripture Worksheet* of Colossians 1 on the following pages, mark these key words: God (as well as synonyms for God), Jesus Christ (as well as synonyms for Jesus Christ), Paul, power, created, and any other repeated words you can find. In the margins, list everything you learn about these words.

2. What other words/and or phrases stand out to you in James 1? Mark these and list everything you learn about them in the margins.

3. Using the *Scripture Worksheet* for Colossians 1 on the following pages, mark the observations listed below using symbols and/or colored pencils.

YOUR OBSERVATIONS? WHAT DO YOU SEE?
1. 5 W's and H 2. Time words. 3. Contrasts. 4. Comparisons 5. Conclusions 6. Cause and Effect 7. General to Particular (vice versa) 8. Progression 9. Lists 10. Title for paragraphs, for chapter

SCRIPTURE WORKSHEET
ALTERNATIVE TEACHING PASSAGE
Colossians 1

1 Paul, an apostle of Christ Jesus by the will of God, and Timothy our brother,

2 To God's holy people in Colossae, the faithful brothers and sisters in Christ:

Grace and peace to you from God our Father.

Thanksgiving and Prayer

3 We always thank God, the Father of our Lord Jesus Christ, when we pray for you, **4** because we have heard of your faith in Christ Jesus and of the love you have for all God's people— **5** the faith and love that spring from the hope stored up for you in heaven and about which you have already heard in the true message of the gospel **6** that has come to you. In the same way, the gospel is bearing fruit and growing throughout the whole world—just as it has been doing among you since the day you heard it and truly understood God's grace. **7** You learned it from Epaphras, our dear fellow servant, who is a faithful minister of Christ on our behalf, **8** and who also told us of your love in the Spirit.

9 For this reason, since the day we heard about you, we have not stopped praying for you. We continually ask God to fill you with the knowledge of his will through all the wisdom and understanding that the Spirit gives, **10** so that you may live a life worthy of the Lord and please him in every way: bearing fruit in every good work, growing in the knowledge of God, **11** being strengthened with all power according to his glorious might so that you may have great endurance and patience, **12** and giving joyful thanks to the Father, who has qualified you to share in the inheritance of his holy people in the kingdom of light. **13** For he has rescued us from the dominion of darkness and brought us into the kingdom of the Son he loves, **14** in whom we have redemption, the forgiveness of sins.

The Supremacy of the Son of God

15 The Son is the image of the invisible God, the firstborn over all creation. **16** For in him all things were created: things in heaven and on earth, visible and invisible, whether thrones or powers or rulers or authorities; all things have been created through him and for him. **17** He is before all things, and in him all things hold together. **18** And he is the head of the body, the church; he is the beginning and the firstborn from among the dead, so that in everything he might have the supremacy. **19** For God was pleased to have all his fullness dwell in him, **20** and through him to reconcile to himself all things, whether things on earth or things in heaven, by making peace through his blood, shed on the cross.

21 Once you were alienated from God and were enemies in your minds because of[g] your evil behavior. **22** But now he has reconciled you by Christ's physical body through death to present you holy in his sight, without blemish and free from accusation— **23** if you continue in your faith, established and firm, and do not move from the hope held out in the gospel. This is the gospel that you heard and that has been proclaimed to every creature under heaven, and of which I, Paul, have become a servant.

Paul's Labor for the Church

24 Now I rejoice in what I am suffering for you, and I fill up in my flesh what is still lacking in regard to Christ's afflictions, for the sake of his body, which is the church. **25** I have become its servant by the commission God gave me to present to you the word of God in its fullness— **26** the mystery that has been kept hidden for ages and generations, but is now disclosed to the Lord's people. **27** To them God has chosen to make known among the Gentiles the glorious riches of this mystery, which is Christ in you, the hope of glory.

28 He is the one we proclaim, admonishing and teaching everyone with all wisdom, so that we may present everyone fully mature in Christ. **29** To this end I strenuously contend with all the energy Christ so powerfully works in me.

OBSERVATION PRACTICE
NARRATIVE PASSAGE

1. Using the *Scripture Worksheet* for Mark 5:21-43, mark the following key words: God (as well as synonyms for God), Jesus Christ (as well as synonyms for Jesus Christ), the bleeding woman, Jairus, Jarius's daughter, Peter, James and John, the crowd, the disciples, etc. In the margins, list everything you learn about these words.

2. What other words/and or phrases stand out to you in this passage? Mark these and list everything you learn about them in the margins.

3. Using the following *Scripture Worksheet* for Mark 5:21-43, mark the observations listed below with the use of symbols and/or colored pencils.

YOUR OBSERVATIONS? WHAT DO YOU SEE?
1. 5 W's and H
2. Time words
3. Contrasts
4. Comparisons
5. Conclusions
6. Cause and Effect
7. General to Particular (vice versa
8. Progression
9. LIsts
10.Title for paragraphs, for chapter

SCRIPTURE WORKSHEET
NARRATIVE PASSAGE
A Dead Girl and A Sick Woman
Mark 5:21-43

21 When Jesus had again crossed over by boat to the other side of the lake, a large crowd gathered around him while He was by the lake. 22Then one of the synagogue rulers, named Jairus, came there. Seeing Jesus, he fell at His feet 23 and pleaded earnestly with Him, "My little daughter is dying. Please come and put your hands on her so that she will be healed and li\ 24 So Jesus went with him.

A large crowd followed and pressed around Him. 25 And a woman was there who had been subject to bleeding for twelve years.

26 She had suffered a great deal under the care of many doctors and had spent all she had, yet instead of getting better she grew worse. 27 When she heard about Jesus, she came up behind Him in the crowd and touched His cloak, 28 because she thought, "If I just touch His clothes, I will be healed." 29 Immediately her bleeding stopped and she felt in her body that she was freed from her suffering.

30 At once, Jesus realized that power had gone out from Him. He turned around in the crowd and asked, "Who touched my clothes?"

31 You see the people crowding against you," his disciples answered, "and yet you can ask, 'Who touched me?'"

32 But Jesus kept looking around to see who had done it.

33 Then the woman, knowing what had happened to her, came and fell at His feet and, trembling with fear, told Him the whole truth. 34 He said to her, "Daughter, your faith has healed you. Go in peace and be freed from your suffering."

35 While Jesus was still speaking, some men came from the house of Jairus, the synagogue ruler. "Your daughter is dead," they said. "Why bother the teacher any more?" 36 Ignoring what they said, Jesus told the synagogue ruler, "Don't be afraid; just believe."

37 He did not let anyone follow him except Peter, James, and John, the brother of James. 38 When they came to the home of the synagogue ruler, Jesus saw a commotion, with people crying and wailing loudly. 39 He went in and said to them, "Why all this commotion and wailing?" The child is not dead but asleep." 40 But they laughed at Him.

After He put them all out, He took the child's father and mother and the disciples who were with Him, and went in where the child was. 41 He took her by the hand and said to her, ""Talitha Koum!" (which means, "Little girl, I say to you, get up!") 42 Immediately the girl stood up and walked around (she was twelve years old). At this they were completely astonished. 43 He gave strict orders not to let anyone know about this, and told them to give her something to eat.

43

OBSERVATION PRACTICE
ALTERNATIVE NARRATIVE PASSAGE

1. Using the *Scripture Worksheet* for Mark 2:, mark the following key words: God (as well as synonyms for God), Jesus Christ (as well as synonyms for Jesus Christ), the paralytic, the crowd, the disciples, the Pharisees, bridegroom, Sabbath, etc. In the margins, list everything you learn about these words.

2. What other words/and or phrases stand out to you in this passage? Mark these and list everything you learn about them in the margins.

3. Using the following *Scripture Worksheet* for Mark 2 on the following pages, mark the observations listed below with the use of symbols and/or colored pencils.

YOUR OBSERVATIONS? WHAT DO YOU SEE?
1. 5 W's and H 2. Time words 3. Contrasts 4. Comparisons 5. Conclusions 6. Cause and Effect 7. General to Particular (vice versa 8. Progression 9. LIsts 10.Title for paragraphs, for chapter

SCRIPTURE WORKSHEET
ALTERNATIVE NARRATIVE PASSAGE

Mark 2

Jesus Forgives and Heals a Paralyzed Man

2 A few days later, when Jesus again entered Capernaum, the people heard that he had come home. **2** They gathered in such large numbers that there was no room left, not even outside the door, and he preached the word to them. **3** Some men came, bringing to him a paralyzed man, carried by four of them. **4** Since they could not get him to Jesus because of the crowd, they made an opening in the roof above Jesus by digging through it and then lowered the mat the man was lying on. **5** When Jesus saw their faith, he said to the paralyzed man, "Son, your sins are forgiven."

6 Now some teachers of the law were sitting there, thinking to themselves, **7** "Why does this fellow talk like that? He's blaspheming! Who can forgive sins but God alone?"

8 Immediately Jesus knew in his spirit that this was what they were thinking in their hearts, and he said to them, "Why are you thinking these things? **9** Which is easier: to say to this paralyzed man, 'Your sins are forgiven,' or to say, 'Get up, take your mat and walk'? **10** But I want you to know that the Son of Man has authority on earth to forgive sins." So he said to the man, **11** "I tell you, get up, take your mat and go home." **12** He got up, took his mat and walked out in full view of them all. This amazed everyone and they praised God, saying, "We have never seen anything like this!"

Jesus Calls Levi and Eats With Sinners

13 Once again Jesus went out beside the lake. A large crowd came to him, and he began to teach them. **14** As he walked along, he saw Levi son of Alphaeus sitting at the tax collector's booth. "Follow me," Jesus told him, and Levi got up and followed him.

15 While Jesus was having dinner at Levi's house, many tax collectors and sinners were eating with him and his disciples, for there were many who followed him. **16** When the teachers of the law who were Pharisees saw him eating with the sinners and tax collectors, they asked his disciples: "Why does he eat with tax collectors and sinners?"

17 On hearing this, Jesus said to them, "It is not the healthy who need a doctor, but the sick. I have not come to call the righteous, but sinners."

Jesus Questioned About Fasting

18 Now John's disciples and the Pharisees were fasting. Some people came and asked Jesus, "How is it that John's disciples and the disciples of the Pharisees are fasting, but yours are not?" **19** Jesus answered, "How can the guests of the bridegroom fast while he is with them? They cannot, so long as they have him with them. **20** But the time will come when the bridegroom will be taken from them, and on that day they will fast.

21 "No one sews a patch of unshrunk cloth on an old garment. Otherwise, the new piece will pull away from the old, making the tear worse. **22** And no one pours new wine into old wineskins. Otherwise, the wine will burst the skins, and both the wine and the wineskins will be ruined. No, they pour new wine into new wineskins."

Jesus Is Lord of the Sabbath

23 One Sabbath Jesus was going through the grainfields, and as his disciples walked along, they began to pick some heads of grain. **24** The Pharisees said to him, "Look, why are they doing what is unlawful on the Sabbath?"

25 He answered, "Have you never read what David did when he and his companions were hungry and in need? **26** In the days of Abiathar the high priest, he entered the house of God and ate the consecrated bread, which is lawful only for priests to eat. And he also gave some to his companions."

27 Then he said to them, "The Sabbath was made for man, not man for the Sabbath. **28** So the Son of Man is Lord even of the Sabbath."

STRUCTURING—ONE MORE HELPFUL OBSERVATION SKILL FOR THE INDUCTIVE STUDY PROCESS

Structuring is a valuable preparation tool, a first step in preparing for studying a book of the Bible. It is a study tool that helps identify the logical flow of a passage, chapter or book of the Bible. As a result, structuring often gives insight into the context, theme and purpose of a passage. It answers the questions "Who? What? Where? When? Why? and How?" Structuring builds your confidence by enabling you to discover the author's intended outline of major and minor points, without inflicting upon the text your own personal prejudice.

RULES FOR STRUCTURING

1. Always write out the text in the order that it is written (NASV strongly suggested because of its close adherence to Greek and Hebrew word order). Don't omit, add or rearrange words.

2. Place the complete thoughts (independent clauses) at the left margin. Independent clauses usually will have a subject (or implied subject such as "you") and a verb.

3. Indent the supporting thoughts (dependent clauses), descriptions of when, where, why, and how and place them directly beneath the word the clause modifies. All dependent clauses should be placed in the middle or the word modified. For example:

> James,
>   a servant of Jesus Christ

4. If a modifier or modifying phrase comes prior to what it modifies, place it above the word being modified, always keeping the text in the order that it has been written. For example:

>   When he asks
> he must believe

5. Place conjunctions or conjunctive phrases **directly** beneath or above the word or phrase they are connecting or contrasting. For example:

> He who doubts is like a wave
>   of the sea
>   blown
>   **and**

6. There is no rigid way to structure but it is possible to be wrong. There are
   several ways that could be correct. For example

Repent   Repent
And each of you   And each of you
Be baptized   Be baptized
     In the name   in the name of JC
       of Jesus Christ   for forgiveness
     for forgiveness   and
and   you will receive
you will receive   the gift of the HS
    the gift
     of the Holy Spirit.

Structuring Sample: James 1:5-8
But
 If any of you
    lacks wisdom
Let him ask of God
      who gives
        to all men
        generously
        without reproach (without finding fault)
and
 it (wisdom) will be given
       to him
 But
Let him ask
    in faith
    without any doubting
      Because the one
        who doubts
          is like the surf
           of the sea
           driven
           and
           tossed
            by the wind.
 For
Let not that man expect
      anything from the Lord,
     Being a double-minded man,
      Unstable in all His ways.

Now the outline for these verses can be clearly seen. The independent clauses at the left hand margin create the outline.

The one who lacks wisdom…..

Let him ask of God

And

Wisdom will be given to him

Let him ask in faith without doubting.

Now it's your turn!

SUMMARY EXERCISE:

Structure Philippians 4:6-7 below or on a separate sheet of paper:

GOAL #1: DEVELOPING BIBLE STUDY CURRICULUM

SECTION B: THE SCIENCE & ART OF ASKING QUESTIONS

COURSE GOAL #1:

This course provides the opportunity for students to:
Learn how to **develop Bible study curriculum** that is biblically sound, relevant, and applicable to all arenas of life.

LIFE TRANSFORMING BIBLE STUDY CURRICULA: IDENTIFYING THE NEED

When choosing or designing Bible study curricula, where do we begin? What is the target on the wall?

- The portion of the B_____we'll study?
- The a_____ and his/her style of writing?
- The amount of h_____we're willing to do?
- The g_____design and the cover?
- The t_____?
- Strong on p_____ reflection ? Or h_____

Or do we begin with. . .
What kind of people are we called of God to produce? Scripture gives us these insights:

> Psalms 1:1-3 His/her delight is in the law of the Lord and on His law he/she meditates day and night. He/she is like a tree planted by streams of water, which yields fruit in season.
> Proverbs 31:30 An individual who fears the Lord is to be praised!
> Isaiah 50:4 He awakes me morning by morning with the ear of a disciple, listening like one being taught.

We are called of God to produce individuals who love God's Word and can study it deeply (and teach it effectively) to bring about life transformation.

> Therefore we should begin by choosing/ designing curriculum that can produce an individual who l_____God's Word and can s_____ it deeply(and t_____ it effectively) to bring about life transformation.

The Unmet Need

Why is excellent targeted Bible study curriculum so difficult to find?

The Problem
- A high percentage of published workbooks are written for an "on-the-spot, no h_____" target group because that's what the m_____ will bear.

Excellent Solutions
- Best "targeted" workbooks on the market: Precepts/Kay and LifeWay/Beth

The "Unresolved Mysteries" of the BS Curriculum Search
- What if your target group wants only 2-3 hours of h_____?
- What if your BS format doesn't allow for a one-hour l_____?
- What if you want to bring a friend who has n_____studied the Bible before but you want to study more in-depth?
- How do you find curriculum targeted for both maximum p_____ enjoyment for the Bible student *and* excellent g_____dynamics?

Satisfied Customer!

| Maximum Enjoyment for Bible Student | + | Excellent Group Dynamics | = |

One More "Unsolved Mystery": How do you meet the temperament differences of Bible students?

THINKERS   **FEELERS**

COED AUDIENCE

50% thinkers 50% feelers

FEMALE AUDIENCE

40% thinkers 60% feelers

How will you meet the needs of both?

What are the necessary ingredients to produce Bible study curricula that results in:

- Maximum personal enjoyment for Bible students
- Excellent group dynamics
- Meeting the needs of both thinkers and feelers
- Meeting the needs of the new Bible student and in-depth learner
- Offering varying homework lengths/depths
- Producing an individual who loves God's Word and can study it deeply (and teach it effectively) to bring about life transformation

The necessary ingredients?

1. Interactive warm-up questions
2. In-depth accurate observation questions
3. Insightful yet accurate interpretation questions based on excellent observation
4. Personal reflective questions that help the text become alive and relevant
5. Excellent correlation questions to correlate the text with other parts of Scripture and relevant life issues
6. Practical measurable application questions that lead to life transformation
7. Multi-level homework in each lesson to allow the new Bible student and the in-depth digger to learn together. For instance:

 Just A Moment Questions (10-15 minutes/day)

 Core Questions (Unmarked questions - 30 minutes/day)

Digging Deeper (45 minutes/day)

Knowing the necessary ingredients will allow you to:

1. **Recognize** them in a Bible Study workbook when evaluating/choosing curriculum
2. **Distinguish** between "the forest and the trees" with published curriculum
3. **Add** missing ingredients to a Bible study workbook to enhance its effectiveness
3. **Create** new curricula/curriculum with all the necessary ingredients

Often evaluating published curricula is a daunting task because it is challenging to know what to look for. We can tend to get lost in the forest of questions and not be able to distinguish between the individual questions or "the forest and the trees." Understanding and being able to recognize the types of questions will aid in selecting and/or evaluation existing Bible study materials.

THE SCIENCE AND ART OF ASKING QUESTIONS

> **"Study the Bible in such a way when we are together, that people can be encouraged to study the Bible on their own as well."**
> **Source unknown**

Remember that the role of the small group leader is to be (1) a stimulator of personal fellowship; and (2) a guide in discovering the truth of God, rather than simply declaring the truth of God. Flow questions can assist you in carrying out each of these roles. There are 5 main types of questions that make up the flow:

- Warm up: "Let's get better acquainted"
- Observation: "What does the text say?"
- Interpretative: "What does the text mean?"
- Correlation: "How does the text correlate with other Scriptures, my life, today's culture or society?
- Application: "How do I respond?"

Flow questions are a series of questions composed and arranged in such a way as to lead a person from *discovering* what a passage says to understanding and applying one or two portions of it to one's daily life in a specific way. The questions are based on one's personal study of the text.

I. Warm-up Questions - A bridge from our world to the Biblical world that accomplishes the goal of "Let's get better acquainted."

A. Developing your warm-up questions
1. Identify the main ideas of a text
2. Choose area(s) on which you will focus the application
3. Choose a warm-up question that will prepare the group for the discussion of that area.
4. Be sure the question has a clear tie to a subject or idea in the text.

56

Example for Philippians 2:5-12: When have you slipped into a role that is not natural to you in order to serve or do something good for someone else?

A. Select warm-up questions that will help the group become better acquainted with one another. For example:
    1. What heroes did you admire as a child? (If studying life of David)
    2. Or, what are the qualities that you appreciate in a friend? (John 15)

B. Warm-up questions can go deeper as the group gets better acquainted; but in the initial stages of group development, warm-up questions should:
1. Be fairly easy to answer.
2. Help people to become comfortable talking with one another.
3. Well-written warm-up questions should allow the Bible study participant to tell a short story.

II. Observation Questions "What does the text say?"

A. Observation questions aim to increase one's knowledge of the text since interpretation, correlation, and application are based on accurate and full observation of what the text says.

B. Observation questions should:
    1. Deal with the key ideas and associated detail germane to the key idea
    2. Take your group into the teaching or events of the passage.
    3. Help the group reconstruct the passage in the words of the text and then in their own words.

C. Do not overlook the observation step:
    1. Even though the answers may appear obvious to you.
    2. Because careful observation provides the foundation for accurate interpretation.
    3. Observation enables appropriate correlation and application.

D. Observation questions should:
    1. Have several answers, each easily discernible from thoughtful reading of the text.
    2. Be chosen so that everyone can participate freely from the outset of the biblical discussion.
    3. **Often use a plural noun** to reinforce several right answers (i.e. insights, blessings, characteristics, promises, commands, etc.)
    4. Avoid one-word answers.

        Example: 1 Corinthians 13
          θ Not - "What never fails?"

Example: Mark 2:1-12

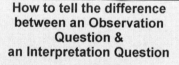

Observation Questions take answers straight from the text.	θ Not – How many friends helped the paralyzed man through the roof? θ But – "What needs did Jesus meet in this passage of individuals and of groups of people?"

A. Determine the number of observation questions by the desired length and depth of the homework (i.e. digging deeper homework may have several more than core question homework).

B. As far as possible:
   1. Use the phrasing of the text in the wording of your questions.
   2. Encourage your group to cite the verse first, then answer in the wording of the text before attempting to paraphrase.
   3. These are especially important if different translations are being used.

III. Interpretation Questions "What does the text mean? (also called Understanding Questions)

A. Interpretation Questions focus on the meaning of the text by enabling you to **draw out implications** or **conclusions** about the text.
B. Interpretation Questions may also **define a word** or its context.
C. Avoid questions that are speculative or unnecessarily controversial:

How to tell the difference between an Observation Question & an Interpretation Question
Observation Questions take answers straight from the text. You don't have to interpret the text. Interpretation Questions you do have to interpret the text.

   1. They can divert and subvert rather than foster spiritual growth and fellowship.
   2. For example, "What did Paul feel like when he apologized to the Corinthians?" (2 Corinthians 1:12-24). If Paul brings this up, then you can. If not, leave it alone.

D. As with the other discussion questions:
   1. Ask questions that promote discussion.
   2. Avoid one-word answers that can close a group down.
   3. Use interpretation questions that require more than a one-word or "yes-or-no" answer.
   4. Reword such questions to change them away from one-word style.
      Example: Not – "Was God pleased with Jonah's response?"
      But – "What does God's handling of Jonah reveal about the character of God?"

IV. Correlation Questions ("How do these ideas compare to other Scriptures, experiences from my life, or today's culture?")

Correlation Questions typically follow an observation or interpretation question and help to clarify or bring deeper or broader insight to the text being studied. There are three types of Correlation Questions:

A. **Scriptural Correlation Questions** – These connect the present passage with other passages in Scripture that help shed light on the present passage.

1. Like observation and interpretation questions, they should have several right answers and promote discussion, even if answers are taken from several different portions of Scripture.

2. They serve as "thinking questions and minister to the "upper levels" of the mind, enabling the Bible student to acquire greater knowledge about the original passage being addressed.

   Example: Philippians 2:5-11 How do the following passages shed shed light on the quality of humility introduced in this passage?

   1 Peter 5 5:8   James 4:9-10   Titus 3:2

3. Scriptural correlation questions typically follow an observation or interpretation question and help to clarify or bring deeper or broader insight to the text being studied.

   For example: Philippians 4:6-7 What elements of Paul's command are suggested as an antidote to anxiety? (Observation Question).

   What insights do the following scriptures give us into why Paul might feel that thanksgiving should be at the front end of any request we make to God? (Scriptural Correlation Question)
   1 Corinthians 15:57 2 Corinthians 2:14 Ephesians 5:20

4. Scriptural Correlation Questions are one of the main tools that can be used to create longer more in-depth homework for Bible participants (Digging Deeper).

B. **Cultural Correlation Questions** – These connect the present passage with perspectives found in our culture or in our world around us. They help us consider how our own thinking has changed or developed since we have met the Lord.

Example: Genesis 4:1-14 To what extent do today's counselors put blame on the environment for bad behavior?

C. **Reflective (Correlation) Questions** - These cause us to take the knowledge of the text and interpret it by reflecting it back into one's life. They help **"life touch life"** and **enable the feeler to "feel involved."**

They connect the biblical world to our world by bringing our lives in review. They **take the discussion to the heart level,** out of the realm of the head and thinking level **through the sharing of personal experience.**

Without them, the **only time "life touches life"** would be at the **beginning of the study** (warm-up question) and at the **end** (application question).

Example: Philippians 4:3-10 "Which of these ideas played a major part in your life when you experienced conflict with another believer?"

Example: Philippians 4:3-10 "How have you personally experienced one of these principles at work on a church committee? In your home? At work?"

They can do one or all of the following (examples from Genesis 1:1-2:3 and Genesis 2:4-5).

a) Enable you to reflect about a **previous life experience** (i.e. *Describe an experience you've had in nature that reminds you of how you would have visualized the earth appearing at its outset?*

b) Enable you to s**hare or reflect your feelings about the knowledge** you have gained from the passage (i.e. *As you look around at God's creation, how does it give you a greater appreciation for the Creator?*)

c) Enable you to **reflect about your present life in light of what you are learning** *(i.e. Note the social dimension of being created in the image of God (v. 18). What implications does this have for your relationships with other people?)*

V. **Application Questions** are designed to help a person apply one's understanding of a passage to daily life in a specific way. Application questions would lead to the exercise of obedience and faith in response to God's truth.

Good Application Questions should lead to the setting of a measurable goal in applying the Word of God. Because it is stated as a question, it still leaves room for the Spirit's leading in individual lives (Example of application which does not leave room for the Spirit's leading; To avoid being conformed to this world (Romans 12:1-2), let's all not use our TV's this week or be on the net.

A. Application Questions yield answers that are:
   1. Measurable,
   2. Achievable within a specific period of time, such as one week or one month.

B. Application Questions remind us that:
   1. Life change comes from obeying the Word of God
   2. We must act, not just know it intellectually.
   3. Two-parted application questions are often needed, one question to narrow to one aspect of the Bible participant's life and the second to narrow to one step or one action to take this week or month.

   Example: Philippians 4:6-7

   θ "What worry will you commit to God in prayer each day this week?"
   θ "What positive step can you take to be faithful in prayer this week for the things that worry you?"

C. Also consider the following in writing and using good Application Questions:
   1. See what application the Biblical writer makes. Translate those into present day terminology.

   2. Sometimes applications can be implemented within the small group itself. "What expression of encouragement would you like to share with another member of the group right now?"

   3. Encourage individuals to share in the group how they tried to apply the previous week's lessons to real life situations. Encourage free expression of failure as well as successes.

   4. Link the sharing of applications with conversational prayer. These are the very areas in which we need one another's prayer, or for which others can join us in praise.

LEARNING TO IDENTIFY GOOD QUESTIONS

Examples of Warm up Questions

Please match each of the following questions with a, b, or c.
a. Warm up Questions too deep for new group
b. A Warm up Question that will NOT lead to personal sharing
c. Excellent Warm up question for a new group

1 Samuel 1—Hannah longs for a child
1. Describe a time when you asked God for something you really wanted and He
   gave it to you. What was it and how did His "yes" answer make you feel?
2. Share a time when you were really depressed. What was the result of your depression?
3. What are symptoms of depression? What do people do when they are depressed?

Examples of Observation Questions

Please match each of the following questions with a, b, or c.
a. Good Observation Question: many answers, will promote discussion
b. Too narrow of an Observation Question: will not promote discussion
c. Not an observation question

Ephesians 1:1-14—Spiritual Blessings from our Heavenly Father
1. What are the spiritual blessings Paul lists in these verses? (List as many as you can). What reasons does Paul give for God having given you these blessings?

        Spiritual Blessings   Reasons

2. Verse 5 reveals that you have been "adopted" by God. According to this verse, why did God "adopt" you?
3. When were the Ephesians chosen to belong to God?
4. With each of these spiritual blessings Paul indicates a time frame in which God gives them (past, present, future). Next to your list of blessings, indicate what you can discover from the text about the timing of the giving of each gift.
5. What words or phrases in this passage reveal Paul's emotions as he is writing?
6. What does it mean to be "blessed in the heavenly realms?" See Eph. 1:20 and 2:6 for additional insight.

Examples of Interpretation Questions

Please match each of the following questions with a, b, or c.
a. Good Interpretation Question: many answers, will promote discussion
b. Too narrow of an Interpretation Question: will not promote discussion
c. Not an Interpretation Question

1 Samuel 1—Hannah longs for a child

1. What do the actions of Elkanah (Hannah's husband) reveal about his character? His capacity to be a good husband?
2. How did Hannah handle the provoking from Pinnenah (Elkanah's other wife)? What steps did she take to cope with her sorrow?
3. Hannah was described as a woman with "bitterness of soul." Is it ever appropriate for a Christian woman to experience such bitterness? Why or why not?
4. Why was Eli's perception of Hannah inaccurate?

Examples of Correlation Questions

Please match each of the following questions with a, b, or c.
    a. Good Scriptural Correlation Question
    b. Good Cultural Correlation Question
    c. Good Reflective (Correlation) Question

Ephesians 1:1-14—Spiritual Blessings from our Heavenly Father

1. When recently have you given a special gift to one of your children (or to a close friend) and have them receive it as a blessing? How did it make you feel?
2. What similarities are there between our spiritual adoption and an earthly adoption? What differences are there between the two?
3. If you have any personal experience with adoption, please share your insights with the group.
4. What additional insights into our adoption by God (v.5) do the following passages give?

        Galatians 3:26-29   Romans 8:15-16
        Galatians 4:5-7   Romans 8:23

Examples of Application Questions

Please match each of the following questions with a, b, or c.

    a. Good measurable, achievable Application Question
    b. Poor Application Question, not measurable or achievable
    c. Not an Application Question

1 Samuel 1—Hannah longs for a child

1. Where in your life right now are you waiting on God? What is one lesson you have learned from Hannah's "waiting room experience" that you could apply to your life? What is one step you could take this week to apply it?
2. What is the one thing that has helped you the most as you have waited on God in the past? Share with us the instance and what you learned from it.
3. .What can you learn from Hannah about how to handle those who provoke you?

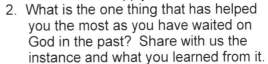

    63

FIXING OUR EYES ON JESUS
Hebrews 12:1-13

"On your mark! Get set! Go!"
Any runner in the starting blocks knows that one of the most deadly mistakes of a competitor is losing one's focus. That was Zola Budd's testimony after running against Mary Decker in the 300-meter finals of the 1984 Olympics. Zola was a promising South African teenage runner who kept a poster of her idol, Mary Decker, on the wall beside her bed. Never did she dream she would someday run against Mary in the Olympics. But in the final heat of the '84 Olympics, they met each other face to face. At about the 1700-meter mark, Decker hit one of Budd's legs, throwing Budd off balance just a bit. Five strides later, they bumped again, causing Budd to land awkwardly. As a result, Decker tripped on Budd's leg, which was thrown out to the side as Budd tried to regain her balance. Then Budd looked back to see her idol falling to the ground.

It was that glance backward that caused Zola Budd to lose her focus and her determination to win. Unfortunately, after years of training and endless hours of discipline, it is often only that inquisitive look that makes the difference between receiving a gold or a silver or a bronze medal.

How important is your focus in life? What effect does it have on your ability to run life's race? Climb into the staring blocks, steady your shaky knees, and fix your eyes on Jesus as you study this passage. The race is winnable with Him as your focus!

1. Name one task you enjoy doing with complete concentration and one in which you tend to get easily distracted.

2. Read Hebrews 12:1-13. According to verse 1, as we run the race of life a "great cloud of witness" is watching and cheering us on. Who are some of these witnesses (see Heb. 11)? In what ways do the lives of three or four of these saints encourage you to keep on running?

   Names of Witnesses   Encourage you to keep running?

3. As we run the race, what actions does the author encourage us to take (Heb. 12: 1-2)?

4. If we are to throw off everything that hinders **and** the sin that so easily entangles, we can assume that sin and hindrances are two different categories. What sins might entangle a Christian as they run the race? What hindrances other than sin might entangle us? (Give several examples of each.)

   Sins   **Hindrances**

In each category, pick one that most often slows you down in your race. How could you throw them off like you would bulky pieces of clothing?

5. What descriptions are given of the One on whom our eyes are to be fixed (vv. 2-4)? Which one of these descriptions most ministers to your own heart right now? Why?

6. In your own words, what do you surmise might be the differences between Christ being the author or our faith and the perfecter of our faith?

   To aid in your understanding of how each role of Christ affects our faith, define each term.

   author of our faith

   perfecter of our faith

7. When the Lord disciplines us, what are two extreme reactions we are cautioned *not* to take (v. 5)?

   Which tends to be your reaction to the disciplining hand of God? Share a recent example.

8. For what reasons does God discipline us (vv. 5-11)?

9. How is God's discipline similar to and different from the way a father disciplines his children (vv. 9-10)?

10. According to the author, how do the short-term aspects of God's discipline compare to the long-term benefits (v. 11)?

11. How have you experienced the Lord's discipline recently?

12. In what ways have you seen the Lord's discipline produce in you "a harvest of righteousness and peace?"

13. In what ways does the author of Hebrews encourage us to cooperate with God's discipline, and why (vv. 12-13)?

14. In your life right now, where are you experiencing a "lame limb," a "weak knee," or a "feeble arm?" (Perhaps your "weak knee" is a fear you need to commit to Jesus, a nagging bad habit, a broken relationship, a neglected prayer life, etc..)

    Pray and ask God to help you "fix your eyes on Jesus" as you turn over this area of discipline to him this week.

65

LEARNING CURVES

THE LEARNING CURVE EFFECT

The learning curve effect states that the more times a task has been performed, the less time will be required on each subsequent iteration.

THE EXPERIENCE CURVE EFFECT

The experience curve effect is broader in scope than the learning curve effect encompassing far more than just labor time. It states that the more often a task is performed the lower will be the cost of doing it. The task can be the production of any good or service.

What implications can be drawn from each of these above effects?

Where are you on your learning curve?

What experience are you bringing to the process?

- o Life experience

- o Previous writing experience

- o Previous curriculum writing experience

- o Previous Bible study experience

NOW IT'S YOUR TURN:
To help you practice how to write **each type of question**, create the following questions for James 1:1-18 **without considering the flow**. Write out brief answers to these questions. Answering your own questions will help you discover the adequacy or inadequacy of each question.

Flow Questions Practice One

One Warm-Up Question
1.

Three Observation Questions
1.

2.

3.

Two Interpretation Questions
1.

2.

Three Correlation Questions (One scriptural correlation question, one cultural correlation question plus two reflective correlation questions)
1.

2.

3.

4.

One Application Question
1.

Now it's time to take the next step in creating a set of flow questions. On the next page, **rearrange your questions into a logical flow**, starting with a warm-up question and ending with an application question. Each interpretation question should logically follow an observation question. Each correlation question should follow either an interpretation question or an observation question. In your set of flow questions, you may or may not include all of the above questions.

To create the flow, you may need to add additional questions not included on this page. As you write, imagine an individual or group gleaning from your questions, as they move logically and/or emotionally from one question to the next.

You may also find it helpful to break these verses into several shorter paragraphs, creating observation, interpretation and correction questions for each section before moving onto the next. Plan on ending with one application question for all 18 verses.

67

Text: James 1:1-18

Major Subject: _____

Flow Questions Practice Two

Write one set of flow questions for the text stated above, ***creating the logical flow as you write.*** Aim to include most of following in your set: one Warm-Up Question, two to three Observation Questions, at least two Interpretation Questions, one Scriptural or Cultural Correlation Question, one Reflective Question, one Application Question, arranged in a logical flow.

1.

2.

3.

4.

5.

6.

7.

8.

9.

10.

FOLLOWING CHRIST'S EXAMPLE
John 13:10-17

"When Dr. Henry Ironside, a great twentieth century Bible expositor, was young boy he helped his widowed mother by working during his vacations, apprenticing himself to a cobbler. It was his job to pound leather for shoe soles. He would take pieces of cowhide, soaked in water, and pound them until they were hard and dry. It was a difficult job, and after endless pounding he would get very tired.

One day he noticed that an ungodly cobbler who worked down the street was not pounding. Instead, he would nail the soles while still wet. When asked why, he responded, "So they will come back quicker." But the Christian owner for whom Henry worked explained to him, "I do not cobble just for 50¢ or 75¢. I do it for the glory of God. In heaven, I expect every shoe returned to me in a pile, and I do not want the Lord to say, "Dan, that was a poor job. You did not do your best."

In John 13, Jesus shows us how even the smallest task can be done for the glory of God and the benefit for others.

1. Describe a recent situation in which someone was a servant to you. What surprised you the most about their servanthood?

2. Read John 13:1-17. According to verse 1-3, what facts did Jesus know about his past, present, and future?

3. In light of this knowledge, why is it surprising what Jesus did next (vv. 4-5)?

   How do Jesus' actions contrast with the way powerful people often treat others?

4. In verses 6-11 Peter and Jesus enter into a debate. What main issues were addressed and who initiated each one?

   Issue?   Who initiated?

5. Why do you think Peter objects to having his feet washed by Jesus?

69

6. What does Peter fail to realize about Jesus' actions and what they symbolize?

7. Although we only need a "bath" from Jesus once, in what sense do we need him to wash our feet each day (vv.8,10)?

8. After washing his disciples' feet, how does Jesus explain the reasons for what he did (vv. 12-17)?

9. Some groups take Jesus' words in verse 14 literally and hold feet-washing services. Yet what are some other specific ways we can serve each other?

10. How has the Lord used you as a "servant" to others recently?

   How were you "blessed" by serving them (v.17)?

11. Christ calls us to follow His perfect example of love by serving each other. What is one way you can serve a fellow believer this week?

   Pray and ask the Lord for wisdom and a servant's heart in following through with your desire.

NOW IT'S YOUR TURN:
To help you practice **how to write each type of question,** create the following questions for Mark 5:21-43 **without considering the flow.** Write out brief answers to these questions. Answering your own questions will help you discover the adequacy or inadequacy of each question.

Flow Questions Practice Three

One Warm-Up Question
1.

Three Observation Questions
1.

2.

3.

Two Interpretation Questions
1.

2.

Three Correlation Questions (One scriptural correlation question, one cultural correlation question plus two reflective correlation questions)
1.

2.

3.

4.

One Application Question
1.

Now it's time to take the next step in creating a set of flow questions. On the next page, **rearrange your questions into a logical flow**, starting with a warm-up question and ending with an application question. Each interpretation question should logically follow an observation question. Each correlation question should follow either an interpretation question or an observation question. In your set of flow questions, you **may or may not include all of the above questions.**

To create the flow, you may need to **add** additional questions not included on this page. As you write, imagine an individual or group gleaning from your questions, as they move logically and/or emotionally from one question to the next. You may also want to consider breaking the passage down into smaller sections (vv. 1-

Text: Mark 5:21-43

Major Subject: _____

Flow Questions Practice Four

Write one set of flow questions for the text stated above, ***creating the logic flow as you write***. Aim to include most of following in your set: one Warm-Up Question, two to three Observation Questions, at least two Interpretation Questions, one Scriptural or Cultural Correlation Question, one Reflective Question, one Application Question.

1.

2.

3.. .

72

THE ART OF ASKING QUESTIONS

> **"Writing is easy - all you do is stare at a blank sheet of paper until drops of blood form on your forehead."**
> **Gene Fowler**

"1. KNOW THE PASSAGE

A. Spend time in the text for your own spiritual benefit. You must hear the voice of God before you lead others in the Word of God. Can a stream rise higher than its source?

B. Identify the major concept or subject of the paragraph and build your questions around it. Hopefully this main idea will meet the most pressing needs of your audience.

Example - Ephesians 1:3-14 "Understanding what God has done for us turns a nobody into a somebody."

C. Identify the main ideas that constitute the major concept or subject. Reflect on their meaning and application.

D. Build questions logically upon one another. Based on these main ideas, move observation, to interpretation, to application as a rule.

E. Stick to the text at hand. Avoid cross referencing in the initial stages of writing your questions. Scriptural correlation questions should be added later, after you have created your basic set of flow questions.

II. DISCERN THE MOST COMMON OR IMPORTANT NEEDS OF YOUR GROUP.

A. Discern needs related to the total person:
1. Physical Needs
2. Mental Needs 3. Social Needs
3. Emotional Needs
4. Spiritual Needs

B. Discern needs related to the five basic psychological needs:
1. Security
2. Love
3. Recognition
4. New Experiences
5. Freedom from Guilt

C. Discern needs that are directly derived from your study of the passage

III. WRITE FLOW QUESTIONS APPROPRIATE TO THE NEEDS OF YOUR GROUP.

A. Select from the passage the concept that most closely relates to their need(s).

B. Select or rewrite observational and interpretive questions which will lead to a discussion of that idea.

C. Follow up with application questions that will motivate each person in the area of need.

D. Write out more questions than you can cover. Usually you can only cover 6-10 questions in 30-45 minutes.

E. Example: Hebrews 10:19-25

Major subject - Being committed to worship responsibilities builds a mature community in the local church.

Example Set of Flow Questions:
1. How has someone spurred you on to love or good deeds in the past month? (WU
2. What exhortations does the author of Hebrews give to Christians? (O)
3. What reasons does the author give for making these exhortations? (O)
4. Who do you know who needs to be spurred on in Christian obedience? (A)
5. What is one way you can spur them on to love and good deeds this week? (A)

IV. GOOD FLOW QUESTIONS (SUMMARY)

5-7 questions for 30 minutes 10-15 questions for 60 minutes

A. Positive Traits – A "Do These" List
1. Each question should have several possible answers.
2. Ask questions that give everyone an opportunity to respond.
3. Formulate questions that focus on the major ideas of the passage. Also have questions on minor parts that bring a sense of newness, illustrate important concepts that we may miss, or that are pre-conditions to fulfilling the main idea.
4. Keep questions short - 17 words or less.
5. Keep questions simple. A question should have only one part to it.
6. Write succeeding questions so they flow logically from a previous one or are in a same set (i.e. observation set).
7. Ask questions that lead to personal involvement.
8. Maintain silence after question is asked. A group needs time to think.
9. Have a proper number of questions for the allotted time:

B. Negative Traits – The "Do Not Do" List

1. Avoid questions that have a "yes" or "no" answer.

2. Avoid questions that have a pre-determined answer.
   - Not, "What are the 4 actions in verses 4-8?"
   - But, "What actions does the author ask people to do in this passage?"

3. Avoid questions that raise unnecessary problems.
   - Speculative or unanswerable – "Where did Cain get his wife?"
   - Doctrinal "Is speaking in tongues normal for today's Christian?"

C. Visualizing the **FLOW** of Flow Questions from **heart** to **head** to **heart** etc.

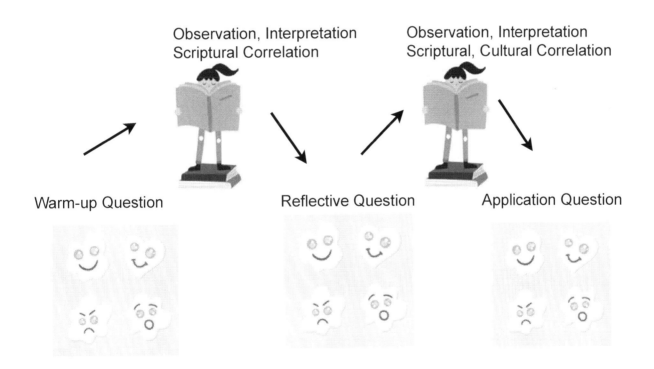

| Observation, Interpretation Scriptural Correlation | | Observation, Interpretation Scriptural, Cultural Correlation |

Warm-up Question   Reflective Question   Application Question

GOOD OBSERVATION QUESTIONS CREATED WITH PLURAL NOUNS

1. Accomplishments
2. Accusations
3. Acts
4. Actions
5. Affirmations
6. Answers
7. Applications
8. Arguments
9. Aspects
10. Attitudes
11. Barriers
12. Behaviors
13. Beliefs
14. Benefits
15. Blessings
16. Celebrations
17. Challenges
18. Characteristics
19. Choices
20. Circumstances
21. Commands
22. Comparisons
23. Compassions
24. Concerns
25. Conclusions
26. Confessions
27. Confirmations
28. Consequences
29. Contrasts
30. Costs/Benefits
31. Creations
32. Curses
33. Dangers
34. Descriptions
35. Desires
36. Differences
37. Discoveries
38. Dissatisfactions
39. Disturbances
40. Effects
41. Elements
42. Emotions
43. Encouragements
44. Essentials
45. Events
46. Evaluations
47. Evidences of belief, unbelief
48. Examples
49. Experiences
50. Expressions
51. Facts
52. Failures
53. Fears
54. Feelings
55. Frustrations
56. Gains
57. Generalities
58. Grievances
59. Guidelines
60. Heart Cries
61. Ideas
62. Images
63. Individuals, Groups of People
64. Inquires
65. Insights
66. Injustices
67. Instructions
68. Images
69. Implications
70. Issues
71. Laments
72. Lessons
73. Longings
74. Losses
75. Messages
76. Methods
77. Modes of communication, travels, etc.
78. Misunderstandings
79. Murmurings
80. Needs
81. Observances
82. Observations
83. Operations
84. Opinions
85. Options
86. Patterns
87. Perspectives
88. Phrases
89. Pleas
90. Points
91. Praises
92. Prayers
93. Problems
94. Proclamations
95. Promises
96. Provisions
97. Purposes
98. Qualities
99. Questions
100. Reactions
101. Realizations
102. Reasons
103. Realities
104. Reassurances
105. Recommendations
106. Records
107. Relationships
108. Requests
109. Requirements
110. Remembrances
111. Resources
112. Responses
113. Responsibilities
114. Results
115. Revelations
116. Satisfactions
117. Scenarios
118. Signs
119. Similarities
120. Sins
121. Solutions
122. Specifics
123. Standards
124. Statements
125. Steps
126. Stipulations
127. Strengths
128. Stresses
129. Struggles
130. Successes
131. Suggestions
132. Summations
133. Teachings
134. Temptations
135. Themes
136. Thoughts
137. Topics
138. Transitions
139. Trials
140. Tribulations
141. Troubles
142. Truths
143. Understandings
144. Upsets
145. Voices
146. Wants
147. Warnings
148. Ways
149. Weaknesses
150. Wonders of God
151. Words
152. Works of the Lord

EXAMPLES OF GOOD INTERPRETATION QUESTIONS

In that curriculum writers have often agreed that good interpretation questions are the hardest type of question to write, please study the following questions to glean insights into how to create good interpretation questions. Notice how they are frequently written as follow ups to observation questions. Also review how they answer one of the questions listed under "types of interpretive questions" when endeavoring to interpret a passage. (see page 19).

Examples of Interpretation Questions	Type of Interpretive Questions
1. **Read Psalm 29:3-9.** In what ways is the voice of the Lord described? (O) 2. Considering the descriptions of the Lord's voice in question 1, what do they indicate about hearing and responding to God's voice? (I)	What does this imply?
1. **Read 2 Samuel 15:22.** What is God's attitude toward obedience? (O) 2. In light of how God views obedience, in Acts 8:26-40, what might have been the consequences to the eunuch as well as to Philip if Philip had not obeyed the voice of the Lord? (I)	How are these related to each other?
1. **Read Psalm 131.** In what ways does David describe himself and the present state of his soul? List as many descriptions as you can find. (O) 2. What does David mean by having a stilled and quieted soul within himself? (I)	What does this word or phrase mean?
1. **Read Psalm 51.** This psalm reveals David's burdened plea to God for mercy. Use a Bible dictionary to define mercy. Given the meaning, what must David have realized about his actions? (I) 2. **Verses 1-2** use a Hebrew technique of synoptic parallelism. In these verses, identify three synonyms for unrighteous behavior and three synonyms for pardon. What significance does David's repetition of the same idea have for you, and what might it suggest about David's present emotional and spiritual state?	What does this imply? What is the significance of this?
1. In the NIV Bible, the phrase "Maker of Heaven and Earth" is used five times. Three of those five times are found in the Psalms of Ascent (Psalm 121:2, 124:8 134:3). 2. Why is the use of the phrase "Maker of Heaven and Earth" in Psalm 121:2 particularly reassuring?	Why is this here?
1. **Read Psalm 123:1,2.** The psalmist states in verse, "I lift up my eyes to You, the One enthroned in heaven." What attitudes are reflected by this statement? In verse 2 the psalmist uses two word pictures. Identify the word pictures. (O) What additional attitudes does each one reflect? (I)	What does this imply?
1. **Read Psalm 136:1-26.** For what reasons does the psalmist give thanks? What acts does God perform that give proof of His enduring love? (O) 2. What characteristics of God are revealed through the above acts? (I)	What does this imply?
1. **Read Psalm 137 and Jonah 2.** Record in the chart below the losses that the Israelites and Jonah are grieving and their heart cry to the Lord. Israelites Losses Being Grieved Heart Cry to the Lord (Psalm 137) Jonah (Jonah 2) 2. In contrasting these situations, do you think the Israelites or Jonah were repentant? Why or why not? (I)	How are these related to each other?

HELPING APPLICATION QUESTIONS GET TO THE HEART LEVEL AND NOT STOP WITH THE HEAD

This exercise is to teach you how to make sure application questions get from the head to the heart. Some application questions require FEELING language to help the Bible student make this transition. Unless something hits us on the HEART level, we can easily ignore the question, choose to skip over it and never apply it to our lives. The goal of application is to move our head knowledge down to our heart and out to our feet and hands.

3C. You have just discovered that dire consequences await those who are unsaved. Who, in your own life, needs to be saved? Commit to praying for this person every day during the coming week. Ask God to open the heart of this individual so that he or she will be open to the truth of salvation.

4C. Perhaps the approach you just described is one that you could take the next time an opportunity arises to share your faith and salvation with the person you identified in question 3C. What specific step will you take to prepare for such an opportunity?

> *4C is a great application question. However, it is written assuming one's heart involvement (on the feeling level) in wanting to take this step.*

The follow-up questions below may help get this application from the head level to heart level:

On a scale of 1-10, how would you rate your **heart-hunge**r for seeing those in your life whn know Christ actually pick up and put on the helmet of salvation?

How can reflecting on the **dire consequences** that await the unsaved (3C) help to create a deeper heart-hunger in you?

What else might help you *really care* about their salvation?

To apply the principles presented in this exercise, please consider doing the following:

After you have written your lesson, review your application questions asking, "Have I helped the Bible participant move this application from the head to the heart? What feeling words could I use in this question or in a follow-up question?

Creating a Five-Day Lesson with Day Titles

Many studies are written as five-day curricula. If we revisit the, "what is the target on the wall" *or"* what kind of individual are we trying to produce," it seems appropriate that we consider him/her to be an individual who is in God's Word on a daily basis. Therefore a Bible study workbook that challenges its students to study five days a week will adequately aim to meet this goal, thus hitting the desired target.

To create a five-day lesson, begin by writing day-titles aimed at creating life-transforming Bible study curriculum. The following principles are helpful in creating a workbook with lessons and day titles that focus on transforming a woman's life.

1. After studying the book of the Bible or chapter(s) to be included in the workbook, divide the book or biblical chapters into the number of desired lessons. Create lesson divisions at natural breaks in the flow of the book of the Bible or biblical chapters to be included in the workbook.

2. Create lesson titles for each lesson, stating each title in terms of personal application to the Bible student. Below are examples of Lesson Titles for "Experiencing God in the Psalms," a nine week study focused on nine types of Psalms.

Lesson One (Ps. 8, 19, 29, 139)
Marveling at God's Creation

Lesson Two (Ps. 131, 23, 8, 3, 46)
Resting in God's Care

Lesson Three (Ps. 27, 42, 43, 63)
Thirsting After God in Times of Stress

Lesson Four (Ps. 1, 51, 73, 18, 90)
Living Out the Psalms' Wisdom

Lesson Five (Ps. 120-134)
Ascending in Praise through the Pilgrim Psalms

Lesson Six (Ps.103, 107, 136, 116, 92)
Increasing in Contentment through Thanksgiving

Lesson Seven (Ps. 55, 137, 18, 62)
Being Real in Victory and Defeat

Lesson Eight (Ps. 45, 22, 2, 110)
Deepening in Love for the Messiah

Lesson Nine (Ps. 40, 71, 78, 92, 96)
Declaring God's Glory

3. Now break down the Scripture for each lesson into five sections, one for each day the student will study.
4. Finally, create day-titles using the same principle utilized for creating the lesson titles. Each day-title should be stated as a personal application to the Bible student. See examples below.

Day One: Psalm 8
Humbled by God's Majestic Creation

Day Two: Psalm 19
Experiencing a Heart Change as a Result of God's Spoken and Silent Revelations

Day Three: Psalm 29
Listening to God's Voice in Creation

Day Four: Psalm 129
Giving Glory to God for His Kingship Over Creation

Day Five: Psalm 139
Praising the Creator and Searcher of My Inmost Soul

Participles (ing words) Helpful in Creating Day and Lesson Title

1. Abiding
2. Acting
3. Affording
4. Aggravating
5. Ascending
6. Attributing
7. Believing
8. Bending
9. Bemoaning
10. Breaking
11. Building
12. Calling
13. Captivating
14. Centering
15. Changing
16. Checking
17. Comforting
18. Committing
19. Confronting
20. Convincing
21. Desiring
22. Crying
23. Declaring
24. Deepening
25. Determining
26. Discovering
27. Discipling
28. Dying
29. Encouraging
30. Enduring
31. Enriching
32. Embracing
33. Exciting
34. Experiencing
35. Exploring
36. Facilitating
37. Falling
38. Feeling
39. Focusing
40. Finalizing
41. Forgiving
42. Fulfilling
43. Giving
44. Going
45. Grasping
46. Growing
47. Guiding
48. Healing
49. Helping
50. Hearing
51. Hiding
52. Hoping
53. Increasing
54. Initiating
55. Inspiring
56. Knowing
57. Leading
58. Legalizing
59. Lifting
60. Listening
61. Living
62. Living out
63. Loving
64. Marveling
65. Meditating
66. Moving
67. Networking
68. Participating
69. Pleasing
70. Praising
71. Receiving
72. Redeeming
73. Resting
74. Restoring
75. Reconciling
76. Remembering
77. Risking
78. Sacrificing
79. Satisfying
80. Seeing
81. Seeking
82. Showing
83. Silencing
84. Sitting
85. Shouting
86. Sleeping
87. Springing
88. Standing
89. Surrendering
90. Taking
91. Testifying
92. Thirsting
93. Touching
94. Thrilling
95. Training
96. Transforming
97. Transitioning
98. Trusting
99. Trying
100. Turning
101. Understanding
102. Upholding
103. Walking
104. Washing

Suggestions for Creating Topical Studies

1. Use all the same types of questions to create a topical study as are used in creating a lesson from a narrative or teaching passage.

2. Keep in mind the desired flow and the need to feed both feelers and thinkers. Therefore start with a warm up, include reflective questions at key "breathing points" throughout the lesson, and end with a measurable, achievable application question. With this "big picture" structure in mind, the only portions of the study that remain are the creation of the observation, interpretation, and correlation questions that fit in between the feeling questions.

3. There are three main ways to create the thinking sections of a topical study:

a. OUTLINE METHOD:
Step One: Construct a word study of the topic, studying all the key Scriptures that relate to the topic as well as related synonyms.

Step Two: From your study of these Scriptures, outline the topic, considering the main themes Scripture teaches on the topic.
For example:

The Justice of God

I. He is Just

    A. In response to the cry of His own heart
       Job 34:12, Gen. 18:25, Is. 59:15-16, 17-18, Ps. 11:7, 5
    B. In response to the cry of the oppressed
       Luke 18:3,5, Ps. 7:6
    C. In response to the cry of the oppressor who wants to stop!
       Is. 59:11

    D. In response to the cry of the those who share God's heart for the oppressed
       Psalm 97:10

II. He is Just
    A. In His time
       Hab. 1;2, Ps. 13:1, Romans 2:4, Ez. 33:11
    B. Now
       Psalm 11:6,7, Rom. 13:1, 1 Pet. 2:23, Is. 53:7, Ps. 37:6, Ps. 23:5

III. He will be Just ...in the End Times
    Jn. 5:22, Rev. 1:18, Rev. 11:15, Rev. 20:12

IV. He was Just – The Just One became the Justifier
    Rom. 3:26, Rom. 5:9

Step Three: Create Correlation Questions that will help Bible students observe what the Bible teaches about each of the main points of the outline.

Step Four: Consider focusing on one or two narrative passages that illustrate one of the main points. Then write observation, interpretation, and correlation questions on this passage. For example, you could take a longer look at Luke 18:1-8, focusing on God being just in response to the cry of the oppressed. In addition, you could take a longer look at Christ becoming our justifier by looking at a gospel account of Christ's death on the cross.

Step Five: Once most of your thinking questions are written, go back and add a warm up, reflective and cultural correlation questions at appropriate places ending the study with a measurable, achievable application question.

b. NARRATIVE PASSAGE METHOD:

Step One: Construct a word study of the topic, studying all the key Scriptures that relate to the topic as well as related synonyms.

Step Two: Help the Bible student begin to address the topic through a narrative passage that adequately addresses the topic. For instance, if the topic is the compassion of God, start your lesson in Mark 5:21-43 (dead girl and sick woman). Write observation and interpretation questions on this passage.

Step Three: Branch out from this passage through correlation questions to different aspects of the compassion of God, such as the timing of His compassion, the objects of His compassion, the limits of His compassion, etc. Add other examples of biblical characters that demonstrated compassion to others, using appropriate questions.

Step Four: Weave in warm up, reflective questions, and a final application question.

c. TEACHING PASSAGE METHOD:

Step One: Construct a word study of the topic, studying all the key Scriptures that relate to the topic as well as related synonyms.

Step Two: Help the Bible student begin to address the topic through a teaching passage that adequately addresses the topic. For instance, if the topic is humility, start your lesson in Phil. 2: 1-11. Write observation and interpretation questions on this passage.

Step Three: Branch out from this passage through correlation questions to different aspects of humility, such as God's love for humility in the Old Testament, God's hatred of pride, the benefits of humility, etc. Also look for biblical characters who demonstrate this quality and create related questions (ie. Moses, Mary, Joseph, etc.)

Step Four: Weave in warm up, reflective questions, and a final application question.

Target Group Assessment for the Creation of Bible Study Workbooks

I. Determine the Purpose(s) of the Target Group's Meeting

A. Primarily for Fellowship centered around the Word?
   Primarily for Growth in In-Depth Bible Study?
   Primarily for Support, Prayer and Worship?

Considering the primary purpose(s) of your meeting, determine the following time frames:

Hours for homework
   1. No Homework – on-the-spot study
   2. Weekly (i.e. 30 minutes, 1-2 hours, 6 hours)
   3. Daily (i.e. 10 minutes, 1 hour)

B. Schedule of Meeting – Time spent in:
1. Prayer
2. Sharing
3. Study of Scripture
4. Social Time
5. Worship

Considering these time frames, determine the shape and length of an individual Bible lesson.
   no homework
   30 minutes of homework
   1-2 hours of homework
   3 hours of homework
   4-5 hours of homework
   3 levels of homework in same lesson
   Just a Moment (10-15 minutes daily)
   Core questions (30 minutes daily)
   Digging Deeper (45 minutes daily)

GOAL #2: SELECTING AND EVALUATING BIBLE STUDY CURRICULUM

COURSE GOAL #2:

This course provides the opportunity for students to:
Acquire skills for **selecting, evaluating, and adapting published Bible study workbooks** for biblical depth, group dynamics, and personal application potentials.

How To Select, Evaluate, and Adapt
Published Bible Study Workbooks

For Biblical Depth:

Establish target group's biblical depth of knowledge **and desire** to learn through surveys, interviews, and direct challenges for spiritual growth.

Check table of contents of workbook for **length of biblical passages** being studied. Some target groups may want to study longer passages, some shorter, depending on their previous experience with God's Word and their desire for growth.

Check the study notes in the back, in the margins, or given as footnotes. These are often **clues to the depth of biblical insight** the author hopes his students will investigate.

Preview one study for its **balance of thinking questions** (observation, interpretation, Scriptural correlation) **versus feeling questions** (warm-ups, reflective and cultural correlation, application). If there is a much higher percentage of feeling questions, the workbook may be shallow in its biblical depth. The author's purpose may not be the grasp of biblical content but rather growth of interpersonal relationships.

Preview that same study answering the thinking questions only. Check for the following insights:

The observation questions have several answers taken **directly from the text.** If true, the author intends students to have good observation skills. If false, the author may not be expecting students to concern themselves with accurate, deep, thorough study of the Word but rather personal reflections generated by the Word.

The interpretation questions call for deep reflection without being needlessly speculative or controversial yet hold potential for promoting discussion.

There are an **adequate number of thinking questions** to generate the **amount of homework** the target group is aiming to complete. Many workbooks on the market today aim for no outside homework prior to class (questions are to be answered on the spot).

For Group Dynamics and Personal Application Potentials:

Evaluate one lesson for its group dynamic potential keeping the following in mind:

Notice the overall pattern of thinking versus feeling questions. Does the study begin at the "heart level" with a warm-up question, proceed to the "head level" with several observation and interpretation questions interspersed with good reflective questions periodically dipping the group down to the heart level? Does the study end with good measurable application questions? Make a diagram of the anticipated "thinking-feeling flow" for the study you are evaluating.

Do the observation questions have several answers, encouraging several people to jump in and answer? If not, it will be difficult to generate good discussion. Far better to find a workbook with a few broad-based observation questions allowing for several answers than many observation questions per lesson but with only one word answers or one or two answers per question. The several answer approach will generate discussion. The narrow one answer type questions will discourage discussion and generate discouragement if wrong answers are given.

Are the warm-ups and reflective questions insightful or trite? Insightful questions will enable a group to be open, vulnerable, and transparent with each other. Trite or too deeply probing questions will shut down the emotional freedom a group has with one another.

Do the application questions generate answers that are measurable, achievable goals within a specific period of time? If they are open-ended and vague or not meant to be shared, the group will be stunted in its ability to grow deep with one another and/or with the Lord.

Are the number of questions to be answered reasonable for the time allowed for Bible study? Too few questions will keep a group from going deep with each other. Too many questions will also discourage deep sharing and interaction, resulting in a hurried desire to simply get through all the questions rather than significantly interact with the text or each other.

Adaptation of Bible Study Workbooks:

It is far easier to adapt a workbook by adding feeling questions than to add observation and interpretation questions. Feeling questions can even be added on the spot to generate deeper personal sharing. Thinking questions are far more difficult to add during the study without generating embarrassment to some Bible study members who have less biblical knowledge and therefore cannot interact as spontaneously.

Therefore I recommend selecting and adapting workbooks with the best possible observation and interpretation questions. It is also much easier to train others to write good warm-ups, reflective and application questions than to train Bible study leaders to write excellent many-answer thinking questions.

Evaluating Bible Study Workbooks

For Biblical Depth
Target Group's Desire
Insights from Table of Contents
Insights from Study Notes
Good or Inadequate Balance of Thinking/Feeling Questions?
Good or Inadequate Use of Thinking Questions?   ➢ Observation Questions (requiring several answers?)   ➢ Interpretation Questions (promote discussion without speculation or controversy?)   ➢ Adequate Number?
Summary and/or Other Insights Related to Biblical Depth

For Group Dynamics
Good or Inadequate Thinking/Feeling "Flow"
Observation Questions (several answers - promote discussion?)
Warm-up and Reflective Questions (insightful or trite, generate vulnerability without probing?)
Application Questions (measurable, achievable, time-related?)
Number of Questions Reasonable for Time Allotment?
Summary and/or Other Insights Related to Biblical Depth?

GOAL #3: TRAINING OF SMALL GROUP DISCUSSION LEADERS

This course provides the opportunity for students to:
Acquire skills in **training Bible study leaders** to be both **effective discussion leaders** and **shepherds**, balancing biblical content with personal group sharing. In addition, students will grow in confidence in **training leaders to grasp principles of leadership** and **leadership character development.**

Section A: Bible Study Administration
Section B. Leadership Skills
Section C. Biblical Skills
Section D. Shepherding Skills

91

GOAL #3: TRAINING OF SMALL GROUP LEADERS

In order for small group leaders to be fully equipped for their ministries, training is needed in the following areas:

- **Bible Study Administration -** In order for a Bible study to grow and thrive it will need both administrative leadership teams and teaching teams. This manual introduces you to examples of necessary job descriptions, procedures and policies needed for creating a successful Bible study administrative and teaching structure. The examples given are only suggestions that can be adapted to your own Bible study structure. Usually small group leaders are given a clear understanding of the administrative structure and the expectations it creates for their successful participation in Bible study at the beginning of the Bible study year (September-April/May. Therefore the documents presented in the first section of this chapter (Bible Study Administration) can be helpful in creating a September training manual for your Bible study leadership.

- **Leadership Skills -** In order for small group leaders to be successful, on going training is also needed in their own view of themselves as leaders. The fourth section of this chapter provides suggested ideas of how to help small group leaders grow in their leadership effectiveness as their own understanding of themselves as leaders also increases.

- **Biblical Skills -** In order for small group leaders to be successful, on-going training is needed in biblical skills. The second section of this chapter provides examples of ways to train leaders in biblical skills.

-

- **Shepherding Skills -** In order for small group leaders to be successful, on-going training is also needed in shepherding skills. The third section of this chapter provides suggested ideas of ways to train leaders to be more effective in their shepherding of those in their small groups.

Before investigating each section, let's consider what leadership training vehicles can best meet the needs of Bible study small group leaders.

WHAT LEADERSHIP TRAINING VEHICLES CAN BEST MEET THE NEEDS OF BIBLE STUDY SMALL GROUP LEADERS?

A. Kick-Off Training in September **(pages 89-112)**

B. Weekly Training/Prayer Options
   1. ½ hour Lesson Review on BS Day
   (i.e. 8:45-9:15 a.m.)
   2. ¼ hour prayer time for BS needs (i.e. 8:45-9 a.m.)

C. Periodic Training
   1. Monthly for elective format mainly for support

   2. November/February for Lecture/Small Group Format

D. Apprentice Training for New Leaders

E. Focus Leadership Training on:
   1. Bible Study Skills (such as given in this manual)

   2. Shepherding Skills

   3. Training in Leadership (i.e. "Leadership" and "Discipleship Magazine," leadership training available from church websites, SHAPE Assessments [Spiritual Gifts, Heart, Passions, Abilities, Personality (Myers-Briggs), Experiences])

   4. Team-Building – a working, supportive, trusting team

Consider: What is our big picture strategy for the on-going training of our leaders?

GOAL #3: TRAINING OF SMALL GROUP LEADERS
SECTION A: BIBLE STUDY ADMINISTRATION

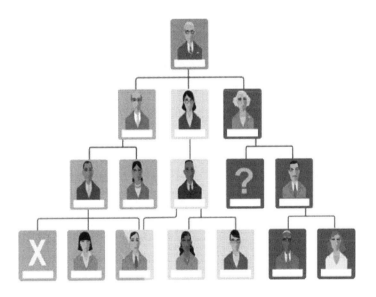

Job Descriptions
Prerequisites
Leadership Commitment
Bible Study
Leadership Team &
Their Teams

Job Descriptions
Prerequisites
Leadership Commitment
Bible Study
Leadership Team &
Their Teams

The following pages provided examples of job descriptions, pre-requisites, etc. often used in a women's Bible study context, although all could be adapted for coed or men's studies as well.

These documents are provided as examples that can easily be adapted for your own ministry settings.

Page 93 provides a suggested strategy for helping a church find ways of encouraging people to understand and respect the differences between volunteer and appointment ministries.

The Commitment on page 103 is provided as a way of encouraging leadership to reinforce Matthew 18 within a ministry setting. All leaders are asked to sign and keep this commitment as a personal reminder of our calling as leaders to commit ourselves to following the principles of Matthew 18 in all interpersonal conflicts and resolutions. .

METRO-WEST WOW CHAIRMAN
Grace Baptist Church
Job Description

GENERAL RESPONSIBILITIES: The Metro-West WOW (Women of the Word) Chairman is responsible for all aspects of MetroWest WOW and reports to the Director of Women's Ministries, or if the Director chooses to fill this position, to an appropriate pastor on pastoral staff.

SPECIFIC RESPONSIBILITIES:

1. To teach approximately 50% of the large group teaching times at WOW.

2. To select and oversee other teachers for large and small group teaching.

3. To select, train, and oversee the training of small group leaders at three yearly training sessions: September, November, and February.

4. To consult and coordinate with other Women's Ministries Coordinators wherever coordination is needed.

5. To develop job descriptions for and to appoint four coordinators to help her in overseeing WOW
   • **First Impressions Coordinator** (oversees details and logistics including hospitality, brunches, name tags, hand outs, gift coordinator, and moderating)
   • **Personnel Coordinator** (oversees people details – registration, directory, publicity, prayer journals, curriculum ordering)
   • **SGL Trainer(s)** - helps to recruit and weekly train small group leaders
   • **Child Care Coordinator** (to oversee childcare workers, programs, etc.) – (May or may not be on the WOW Leadership Team, depending on whether she is Child Care Coordinator for just WOW or also for other Women's Ministries weekly events).

Sets budget and approves all expenditures.

Meets periodically with treasurer for accountability of budget.

If not also the Director, functions as a member of the Women's Ministries Team.

TALENTS, GIFTS, SKILLS QUALIFICATIONS HELPFUL IN THIS ROLE:
1. Capable and maturing Christian.
2. Attends and calls Grace Baptist Church her church home.
3. Solid grasp of Scripture and sufficient skills for large and small group teaching.
4. Husband's approval and encouragement to serve (if applies).
5. Organized thinker and ability to visualize people's giftedness and delegate accordingly.
6. Complete understanding of and agreement with church doctrine and philosophy of ministry.
7. Desire to see women come to a trusting relationship with Christ.
8. Meets pre-requisites for small group leaders.

VOLUNTEER VS. APPOINTMENT MINISTRIES POLICY

Volunteer Ministries: Most ministries of the church are volunteer ministries, ministries which individuals are free to offer to participate in.

Appointment Ministries

1. Defined by Scripture as ministries for which one cannot not volunteer but must wait to be asked to participate in. Many leadership ministries are considered to be appointment ministries.

2. Scriptural pattern for appointment ministries assumes that leaders are gifted and called by the Holy Spirit to appoint other leaders (Acts 6:1-4, Titus 1:5, Acts 14:23, 2 Tim. 1:11, Ex. 18, 2 Tim. 2:2).

3. The Scriptural pattern for such ministries also includes specific spiritual qualifications given as guidelines to aid leaders in choosing other leaders (1 Tim. 3:1-13).

4. In addition to Scriptural qualifications, the Holy Spirit's divine guidance is needed as the leader prays and waits on God to reveal who should be appointed to these ministry positions (Mk. 3:13, Acts 13:2-3, Acts 6:1-4, Eph. 2:10).

5. Since it is the Holy Spirit who ultimately gifts and calls individuals to certain ministries, it is important for the spiritual leader to be asking the Holy Spirit to reveal who He is ultimately calling to these ministry appointments (Jeremiah 1:5,10; Acts 13:2-3).

6. Staff in charge of a particular ministry determines which ministries are to be designated appointments and which volunteers can fill. However, most volunteer ministries should also have job descriptions listing job qualifications.

VS

METROWEST WOW SGL TRAINER
Grace Baptist Church
Job Description

GENERAL RESPONSIBILITIES: The MetroWest WOW Small Group Leader Trainer(s) are responsible to assist the WOW Chairman, or the Director of Women's Ministries (if she chooses to fill this position), in the training of the small group leaders for WOW. They are directly responsible to the MetroWest WOW Chairman/Director of Women's Ministries.

SPECIFIC RESPONSIBILITIES:

1. To lead the small group leaders through a weekly lesson review held at the start of each WOW session, alternating with other WOW SGL Trainers.

2. To create a training schedule and supply it to the WOW Chairman.

3. To oversee emailing of the Leader's Sheet to all small group leaders, AM and PM.

4. To aid in the selection and recruitment of next year's small group leaders in conjunction with the MetroWest WOW Chairman. Recruitment should take place within the final weeks of the Bible Study year in preparation for the fall.

5. To give feedback to the WOW Chairman regarding training needs in preparation for the three yearly training sessions: September, November, and February.

6. To aid in the selection of WOW curriculum in close coordination with the WOW Chairman and appropriate PM WOW small group leaders or/trainers.

7. Meets periodically with WOW Leadership Team for personal sharing, prayer, planning and administrative coordination.

TALENTS, GIFTS, SKILLS QUALIFICATIONS HELPFUL IN THIS ROLE:
1. Capable and maturing Christian.
2. Attends and calls Grace Baptist Church her church home.
3. Solid grasp of Scripture and an ability to teach.
4. Husband's approval and encouragement to serve (if applies).
5. Excellent skills in large and small group teaching.
6. Organized thinker and ability to visualize people's giftedness and delegate accordingly.
7. Complete understanding of and agreement with church doctrine and philosophy of ministry.

METROWEST WOW JOB DESCRIPTION
SMALL GROUP CO-LEADERS

1. **SHEPHERD THE MEMBERS OF YOUR SMALL GROUP.** This includes maintaining regular contact with group members through phone calls or note writing; and encouraging members of the group to minister to each other and to their non-Christian friends and neighbors.

2. **ATTEND PRAYER TIME ON MORNINGS NOT LEADING** (8:45 to 9:00 a.m.) geared for prayer and support for the morning's study in Prayer Room.

3. **ATTEND TRAINING TIME ON MORNINGS LEADING** (8:45 to 9:15 a.m.) geared to equip you to lead your small group and answer any questions about the lesson.

4. **LEAD THE WEEKLY MEETING** (9:28 to 10:45 a.m. 1/3 of time prayer requests/ 2/3 lesson) **AND BE RESPONSIBLE TO LEAD AND CHALLENGE YOUR SMALL GROUP TO BE ON TIME FOR WORSHIP/LECTURE (10:50-11:30 a.m.)**

5. **ATTEND SMALL GROUP LEADERS MEETINGS (Time TBA).** The focus of these times is to gain further training as well as to continue to build our unity as small group leaders of WOW.

6. **SHEPHERD GROUP MEMBERS OUTSIDE OF WEEKLY MEETING.** As the Spirit leads, please contact your women by email or by phone to help build personal relationships with them during the Bible study year. You may want to divide the list with your co-leader.

7. **WORK AS A TEAM WITH CO-LEADER AND CONNECTION COORDINATOR.** Serve as prayer partners for the women in your group, share in the shepherding, and alternate in discussion leadership.

8. **PRAY REGULARLY FOR WOMEN IN YOUR SMALL GROUP.** Prayer will be the strength of your ministry. It will provide you with wisdom for counseling, motivation to keep caring, and the discernment in balancing this ministry with your calling as a wife, mother, neighbor, etc.

9. **CALL YOUR CO-LEADER TO LET HER KNOW SHE IS LEADING IF YOU ARE UNABLE TO BE AT WOW.** Should your co-leader be out of town or unable to attend, please call the Small Group Trainer Coordinator. IF YOU ARE UNABLE TO ATTEND, ALSO PLEASE CALL 978-562-8550 extension 126 and leave a message signaling your absence, in addition to informing your co-leader.

10. **ATTEND YOUR SMALL GROUP FALL and SPRING LUNCHEONS.** Luncheons will be scheduled in the middle of the semester, with child care available at the church. Groups may want to go out to lunch or decide to take salads or sandwiches to a member's home. Enjoy!

TALENTS, GIFTS, SKILLS, QUALIFICATIONS NECESSARY IN THIS ROLE:

1. A love for God's Word and a desire to teach and shepherd His people.
2. Attendance at and consideration of Grace Baptist Church as your home church.

PREREQUISITES FOR SMALL GROUP LEADERS

A small group functions as a caring loving family unit that creates an environment for spiritual growth as well as for introducing the non-Christian to Christ. In a similar way, the Small Group Leader functions as a shepherd, discipler, and evangelist within her group. It's not necessary to have every existing skill and gift, but the following characteristics are helpful:

1. **BE A THREE PRIORITY PERSON** - The following three priorities describe a balanced Christian life:
   A. **A growing commitment to Jesus Christ** and His Word. However, it is not necessary to be a spiritual giant in order to be a Small Group Leader. This priority does not have as much to do with where we are as with the direction we are moving.
   B. **A growing commitment to the Body of Christ**. This should first be expressed by his/her commitment to family. In the case of a single, his/her relationships with his/her roommate and parents should be healthy. As he/she relates to the Body of Christ outside his/her home, he/she should be willing to illustrate the "one anothers" of scripture - to love, encourage, build up, exhort, etc. He/she should be willing to express this commitment through regular attendance at our church's Sunday morning worship service. He/she needs to demonstrate a team spirit and a willingness to follow the direction of spiritual authority (see Hebrews 13:17)
   C. **A growing commitment to the work of Christ in the world** including a concern for social needs, missions, and a special concern for participants in his/her small group.

2. **BE FAITHFUL, AVAILABLE, TEACHABLE AND STABLE**
   A. **FAITHFUL.** This is the ability to follow through on commitments. Scripture indicates that faithfulness is demonstrated first in the home as Titus 2:5 indicates and as Proverbs 31 demonstrates. It is then demonstrated by one's willingness to consistently meet with the Body of Christ (Hebrews 10:24-25).
   B. **AVAILABLE.** To seriously seek to serve those in your small group will cost time and energy.
   C. **TEACHABLE.** This is a deep desire to know God and to do His will. It is an orientation toward being a doer of the Word and not just a hearer. It also involves a genuine willingness to seek the counsel and correction of those around her (see James 1:22, Proverbs 12:15,19:20)
   D. **STABLE.** While we all go though emotional ups and downs, the Small Group Leader should not be subject to deep or lasting periods of depression. He/she must illustrate self-control and endurance even during the difficult times.

3. **BE CALLED BY GOD.**
   Nothing is more exciting, challenging, and frustrating than ministering to others. Without assurance of God's call, you may be tempted to quit. The following questions may help:
   A. Do I meet the prerequisites of a small group leader?
   B. Am I willing with God's help to fulfill the job description of a Small Group Leader?
   C. If married, have I discussed the prerequisites and job description with my

106 September Training: Bible Study Administration

METROWEST WOW JOB DESCRIPTION
SMALL GROUP CONNECTION COORDINATOR

RESPONSIBILITIES:

1. **ASSIST YOUR SMALL GROUP LEADERS IN SHEPHERDING THE WOMEN OF YOUR GROUP.** This includes following up on absentees, and generally getting to know the women in your group. When calling those who are absent, the following suggestions may be helpful:
   a. Let her know she was missed. Show interest in the events of her life without prying.
   b. Share one key element from your class, either a prayer request or some key point discussed, or some key insight from the lecture.
   c. Ask her if she has a prayer request and offer to pray for her in the coming week.
   d. Let her know of any upcoming events that could help her feel connected when she returns to WOW (i.e. next week's lesson number, the small group luncheon date, etc.)

2. **ASSIST YOUR SMALL GROUP LEADERS BY TAKING ATTENDANCE WEEKLY ON THE ATTENDANCE SHEET PROVIDED IN YOUR BASKET.**

3. **ATTEND TO DETAILS RELATED TO YOUR SMALL GROUP'S LUNCHEON/SOCIAL (Fall/Spring) SUCH AS:**
   a. Oversee the provision of map for lunch/social location (i.e. ask hostess to provide, OR provide directions to small group members from MapQuest, etc.)
   b. Facilitate an accurate childcare count from the moms in your small group to be given to the child care coordinator one week prior to luncheon/social (i.e. facilitate completion of child care sign-up sheet by moms during small group, call WOW absentee moms and ask if they need child care for luncheon/social, etc.)

4. **ASSIST SMALL GROUP LEADERS WITH CHRISTMAS GIFTS AND/OR END OF THE YEAR GIFTS FOR GROUP MEMBERS, IF DESIRED.** Gifts should be small and inexpensive to keep from fostering competition between small groups.

5. **OFFER TO BE A PRAYER PARTNER FOR YOUR SMALL GROUP LEADERS.**

108 September Training: Bible Study Administration

COMMITMENT

I accept the challenge of commitment to the MetroWest WOW Leadership for a ONE-YEAR period. Before God I pledge to do the very best that He gives me the ability to do and to be faithful in my responsibilities. I understand and accept that leadership carries an accountability to be an example with my life and words in the following ways:

- I will maintain a regular quiet time of study in the Word and prayer as a foundation for ministry to those in my small group.

- I will maintain a positive attitude toward pastors, church leadership and fellow team members of our Bible Study.

- I will work for the unity and understanding among my brothers/sisters and will not hold a grudge when offended. If I should have trouble dealing with an offense, I will go to my brother/sister, and not talk to others, so that I may resolve the situation and thereby continue to love in unity. I will follow the biblical instructions in Matthew 18:15 for resolving difficulties.

- I will make my attendance at worship services a priority.

- I will maintain a teachable attitude with my spiritual leaders, opening up to the benefit of the checks and balances of godly counsel and lifestyle integrity.

- I accept responsibility to continually uphold this ministry in prayer, that God's Spirit will be released to change lives and that Jesus Christ alone will be exalted in everything we do.

Name _____

Date _____

Sign here

PRE-DETERMINED TEAM DECISIONS THAT SHAPE WOW PHILOSOPHY

This document can be helpful when new leaders are added who don't know WOW's history. Creating a similar document for your ministry setting may help new leaders become more quickly in tune with present leadership.

Decision/Rationalizations/Advantages	Which Team?
1. WOW CURRICULUM PHILOSOPHY **A. ONE TRACK – rather than 5 tracks** 1) Ease of leadership training 2) Ease of multiplication of leadership 3) Ease of multiplication of small groups and numerical growth 4) Ease of quality control of curriculum and curriculum development	WOW SGLer's '02-'03
B. 3 LEVELS OF STUDY - Just a Moment, Core, Digging Deeper 1) Older women teaching younger women (Titus 2) 2) New believer/seeker with long time believer/Bible student 3) 1st time WOW participant with long-time WOW participant 4) Busy participants (Just a Moment) with those who Dig Deeper	WOW SGLer's '02-'03 CW Team '08
C. 5 DAYS OF HOMEWORK 1) Target on wall of the kind of individual we feel called of God to produce: A person developing a daily walk with Christ through inductive study 2) Therefore time in small group requires flexibility – can't cover every question. Must choose wisely questions covered to interest and challenge all 3 levels of participants.	WOW SGLers '02-'03
D. CURRICULUM WRITTEN BY CWT AS PACE-SETTER FOR CURRICULA 1) CWT has limited writing capacity (at most 10 out of 22 lessons) 2) Other curricula chosen w/ CWT's criteria in mind as much as possible	CWT

E. WOW - A BIBLE STUDY MORE THAN A SUPPORT GROUP
1) Request your participation in entire program as requested
  a. Balance of time in small groups on BS (2/3) vs prayer requests (1/3)
  b. Leading your small group to full/on-time participation in worship/lecture
	Small Group Leadership Challenge of Spring '08 CWT '08

F. WOW CURRICULA YEARLY CHOICES 1) Chosen by Spirit-led process with Lecturing Team's interactive participation 2) Chosen with GBC's Big Picture Vision in mind (i.e. Becoming a Woman of Compassion)	Lecturing Team Suggestions welcome from SGLer's with CWT's criteria in mind
2. GRACE BAPTIST CHURCH'S LONG RANGE PLANNING PHILOSOPHY Mission Statement – to know and grow in Christ, to go and show His love **10 GBC Values** **Christ-centered Worship (CW)** **Healthy Families (HF)** **Biblical Instruction (BI)** **Prevailing Prayer (PP)** **Authentic Community (AC)** **Personal Evangelism (PE)** **Global Impact (GI)** **Loving Service (LS)** **Servant Leadership (SL)** **Cultural Relevance (CR)**	GBC'S Envisioning Leadership Team '07-'08

SCHEDULES

WEEKLY
BRUNCH/DESSERT

Pages 109-11 provide examples of possible schedules for morning women's Bible studies and brunches. They are provided to stimulate your own creativity for ideas within your own ministry settings.

Since many participants in a curriculum writing class often write curricula for women's studies, these examples of morning schedules are provided to answer many of the questions that often arise from women taking this class.

Tuesday A.M. MetroWest Weekly Schedule
for Small Group Leaders and WOW Leadership Team

8:40 Arrive in Building to deliver children to child care

8:45 – 9:15 On teaching weeks, attend lesson review in hospitality room

8:45 – 9 On non-teaching weeks, attend prayer time in prayer room

9 WOW Begins – pick up name tags from baskets, refreshments from tables, welcome friends and newcomers

9 – 9:20 Refreshments

9:20 – 9:25 Announcements
> If you have an announcement, please email or phone in announcements to Bible Study Chairman no later than Monday morning at 10 a.m. Announcements restricted to women's events and selected all church events and/or opportunities particularly pertinent to WOW women and their families.

9:25 – 10:45 Small Groups / Take Baskets to Small Groups

Use of Baskets for Communication with Small Group Leaders
> BS participants locate name tags in small group baskets in hospitality room
> Small group leader take basket to class for name tags for late comers and handouts
> Return baskets to lecture room prior to lecture
> Name tags back in small group baskets at end of lecture
> Christmas Ticket Sales
> Retreat Flyers
> Any other handouts related to Women's Ministries or All-Church Events

10:40 Door Knock as warning to end Small Group Time

10:45 Leave small group room and proceed to Lecture

10:45 – 10:50 Travel Time

10:50 – 11 Praise and Worship

11 – 11:30 Lecture

11:30 Dismissal

PLEASE RETURN BASKETS TO Room 113-117 at end of WOW Morning

FYI-Alternative schedule - opening first, then go to small groups.

     September Training: Bible Study Administration

WOW Opening Brunch Schedule
September 15, 2009

8:45 a.m. Prayer with small group leaders in room 112

9:00 Informal welcome and greeting of women

9:20 Formal welcome, door prizes, prayer for meal, question to share over meal "Something fun I did this summer was" AND…"In what way do you feel you 'blossomed' this summer?"

10:10-10:30 Announcements and Administrative Details	Phyllis
10:30- 10:50 Worship	Nancy Jean
10:50 – 11:30 Introduce theme and curriculum for year	Phyllis

WOW Opening Dessert Schedule
September 15, 2009

6:30 p.m. Prayer with small group leaders in Women's Ministries Office

6:40 – 7:05 Informal welcome and greeting of women

7:05 – 7:10 Formal welcome, door prizes, prayer for dessert   Phyllis
Formal welcome, door prizes, prayer for meal, question to share over meal "Something fun I did this summer was" AND…"In what one way do you feel you "blossomed" this summer?"

7:50 – 8:05 Announcements and Administrative Details	Phyllis
8:05-8:25 Worship	Lynn
8:25-8:55 Introduce theme and curriculum for year	Phyllis

Example of Small Group Placement Card

Name: _____ Phone: _____

Ages of Children:_____ Town: _____

Study Level: Just a Moment ( )   Core ?'s ( )

I would like to be placed in a small group with:

_____

_____

I would like to be in the Early Bird group_____ OR Regular Time _____

I will be bringing a nursing baby: yes ( )   no ( )
I would prefer a group WITHOUT a nursing baby   yes ( )   no ( )

I have the following special needs: _____

Name: _____ Phone: _____

Ages of Children:_____ Town: _____

Study Level: Just a Moment ( )   Core ?'s ( )

I would like to be placed in a small group with:

_____

_____

I would like to be in the Early Bird group_____ OR Regular Time _____

I will be bringing a nursing baby: yes ( )   no ( )
I would prefer a group WITHOUT a nursing baby   yes ( )   no ( )

I have the following special needs: _____

Name: _____ Phone: _____

Ages of Children:_____ Town: _____

Study Level: Just a Moment ( )   Core ?'s ( )

I would like to be placed in a small group with:

_____

_____

I would like to be in the Early Bird group_____ OR Regular Time _____

I will be bringing a nursing baby: yes ( )   no ( )
I would prefer a group WITHOUT a nursing baby   yes ( )   no ( )
I have the following special needs: _____

GOAL #3: TRAINING OF SMALL GROUP LEADERS

SECTION B:
LEADERSHIP SKILLS

119

Leadership is Influence–nothing more, nothing less.

John Maxwell

Leadership is perceiving where Christ is taking His people.

Tom Erickson

If you perceive yourself as chosen of God, you will make an impact.

Howard Hendricks

Leadership is deciding once and for all who will get the glory,
you or God.

Author Unknown

My dear children, for whom I am again in the pains of childbirth until Christ is formed in you. Galatians 4:19

The Apostle Paul

Not so with you. Instead, whoever wants to become great among you must be your servant, and whoever wants to be first must be slave of all. For even the Son of Man did not come to be served, but to serve, and to give his life as a ransom for many. Mark 10:43-45

SMALL GROUP DYNAMICS

FACILITATING A BIBLE DISCUSSION

BE PREPARED!!

1. Pray for the ability to guide the discussion with love and understanding.

2. Always have your homework completed. If you are unable to do this, please have someone else lead (i.e. co-leader).

3. Familiarize yourself with the study questions until you can rephrase them in your own words. Be careful however, to not lose everyone by your rephrasing. You might want to read the question as is, and then rephrase it.

4. Timing - Begin and end on time. You will encourage participants to wander in late if you wait for everyone to arrive before starting. Time out the lesson. Place the anticipated time in the margin next to key questions so you know whether you are getting behind as you lead through the lesson.

5. Prepare the situation by:
   a. positioning people wisely. (Beware of lining up all the Christians across from all the non-Christians or all the verbal ones across from all the quiet.)

   b. getting rid of extra chairs. Empty chairs destroy intimacy.

   c. making sure that everyone can see everyone else.

6. General flow of small group:
   a. Prayer period
      The prayer period should begin by 9:30a.m./7:45 p.m. with the writing out of prayer requests on prayer cards. Share prayer requests and then pray. Plan to finish the prayer portion of your small group no later than 9:55a.m./8:05 p.m.

   b. Warm-up period
      Use of a warm-up question can often help bring needed warmth to a group so they can be ready to share more intimately (see examples of good warm-up questions).

   c. Example of a suggested Discussion Period for a Morning Bible study with lecture at end of the morning.
      Take your participants through the lesson, feeling free to add your own questions and subtract questions as you sense the needs of your group. If you choose to delete questions, allow time at the end for someone to ask a question about something you deleted. The warm-up and discussion periods should take about 40 minutes.
   A final prayer period should begin 10:30/8:50 with the sharing of answers to the application question. Share in 2's and then come back together for prayer.

7. Consider the overall flow of your lesson in adding and deleting questions.

8. Do not linger too long over any one question. Place the time in the margin of your book so you know whether you are on target or running a little late. Use 9:35, 9:40, 9;45, rather than 10 minutes, 5 minutes etc. If the discussion goes too long on a question, be prepared to delete a question or two to catch up.

9. Application questions open a group up to one another and keep them focused on personal sharing rather than just wanting prayer for their "aunt's dog who is dying". After many have shared an answer to the application question, additional prayer requests can be taken.

10. In most Bible studies where prayer requests are taken after the study of God's Word, the Bible is closed and requests are taken that have nothing to do with the passage just studied. As a result, we lose the work the Spirit has just accomplished in the lives of small group members. Prayer requests in this type of Bible study are often shallow and not life changing.

   Studying the Bible peels back the protective layers we use to hide from one another. An application question coming out of the passage just studied can help us take the truth of God's Word and walk it into our lives in a very practical way.

11. Encourage your participants to keep all prayer requests (from application questions as well as additional requests) in the prayer notebooks provided. Prayer notebooks can be tucked inside of the Bible study workbook and used during the week to enhance personal prayer times.

12. Encourage small group participants to bring their prayer notebooks with them to the small group and fill them out during the prayer time (with eyes open - it really is OK with the Lord!!). This will encourage participants to have the opportunity to pray for one another during the week rather than just during small group.

13. Encourage everyone to participate in the discussion and in prayer by:
    a. Receiving all answers warmly. Never bluntly reject what anyone says, even if you know the answer is incorrect. Instead ask "Where did you find that?" or "What do some of the rest of your think?" Allow the group to handle problems together. Try not to be the antagonizer. Let others in the small group be the corrector of errors as much as possible.
    b. Encourage the quieter ones to participate in prayer with the use of one word prayers of praise for who God is, by asking for volunteers for specific requests, or with the use of sentence completion prayers such as:
    Lord, you are _____. .
    Lord, thank you for _____.
    Bless _____ with her family this week.
    Bless _____ in her job this week.
    Help _____ in her prayer time.
    Help _____ in her time in the Word.
    When people learn to pray first with a structure, they soon feel comfortable praying without a structure. These techniques can be particularly helpful at the beginning of the year as a small group is getting acquainted.

14. Be sure you do not talk too much. As the leader, your role should be as moderator or as a conductor, keeping the group on the subject being discussed. You be the question asker, letting them give the answers. Bring them back on the track if they get off the original subject.

127

. Don't always wait for someone to volunteer their answers. Feel free to call on your participants, unless it is a highly personal question. Keep the tempo of your class moving.

15. Watch hesitant members for an indication by facial expression or body posture that they have something to say. Give them an encouraging nod or speak their name.

16. Tactical difficulties: How to handle the:

a. Derailer - whose comments lead the group off track.

1. Remind her of the topic being considered.

2. Say, "That's an interesting question, but we really don't have time to deal with it now. Let's talk about it together over the phone this week/after Bible study."

b. Monopolizer - who does most of the talking, thereby preventing others from sharing.

- Don't sit across from them. Have them 1/4 of the way round the circle off to your left or right. The second most powerful person in a group is the person sitting across from the leader. Every time you look up, you give them permission to speak. Your co-leader probably should not sit there either. It could put her in the position of feeling obligated to answer all your questions and thereby killing group discussion.

- Break down into smaller groups. This keeps the problem localized.

- Before opening up time for sharing say, "We only have about 5 minutes for this question, so everyone limit your remarks to 1-2 minutes."

- After he/she has shared say, "Now let's hear from some others", or "Do any of the rest of you have any insight here?"

- Talk with him/her outside of your small group. Get him/her on your team. Say to her, "I'm having trouble getting through the lesson on time. Could you help me by keeping an eye on the clock so we can move a little faster?" Or say, "You seem to have a lot of insight. How do you think we could get the others gals more involved in the discussion in small group? We seem to have such a quiet group."

c. **Timid Person** – who feels most comfortable when she is not sharing.

1. Ask a question in which everyone can be encouraged to give an opinion, such as "What type of recreation do you enjoy most?" Without pressuring her, ask her by name an easy question or one having several answers.

2. Express appreciation for his/her contribution when she does share.

d. **Pre-Christian**

- Love him/her, pray for him/her, call him/her, validate his/her questions 'What a great question!"

- Allow the group to help correct his/her misconceptions as much as possible so that you can help maintain your relationship with him/her as his/her leader.

- When you need to correct say, "You almost have it..." or "That is a helpful insight, but I think the Bible might more accurately communicate that...."

- If you cannot answer his/her question, thank her for asking it and say, "That's a great question. I'll need to do some research and get back to you on that one."

- For the prayer time remind them:

a. There is NO PRESSURE to pray. "You can pray when you feel ready."

. For the prayer time remind him/her:

a. There is NO PRESSURE to pray. "You can pray when they feel ready."

b. Prayer requests are optional. "If you have a concern, we'd love to pray for you."

GOD LOVES IRREGULAR PEOPLE TOO!

a. **DERAILER** - whose comments lead the group off track.
   1. Remind him/her of the topic being considered.
   2. Say, "That's an interesting question, but we really don't have time to deal with it now. Let's talk about it together over the phone this week." or "after Bible study."

Our derailer tends to be:

b. **MONOPOLIZER** - who does most of the talking, thereby preventing others from sharing.
   - Don't sit across from him/her. Have them 1/4 of the way round the circle off to your left or right. The second most powerful person in a group is the person sitting across from the leader. Every time you look up, you give him/her permission to speak. Your co-leader probably should not sit there either. It could put him/her in the position of feeling obligated to answer all your questions and thereby kill group discussion.
   - Break down into smaller groups. This keeps the problem localized.
   - Before opening up time for sharing say, "We only have about 5 minutes for this question, so everyone limit your remarks to 1-2 minutes."
   - After he/she has shared say, "Now let's hear from some others", or "Do any of the rest of you have any insight here?"
   - Talk with him/her outside of your small group. Get him/her on your team. Say to them, "I'm having trouble getting through the lesson on time. Could you help me by keeping an eye on the clock so we can move a little faster?" Or say, "You seem to have a lot of insight. How do you think we could get the others gals more involved in the discussion in small group? We seem to have such a quiet group."

Our monopolizer tends to be:

c. **TIMID PERSON** - who feels most comfortable when she is not sharing.

   - Ask a question in which everyone can be encouraged to give an opinion, such as "What type of recreation do you enjoy most?"
   - Without pressuring her, ask her by name an easy question or one having several answers.
   - .Express appreciation for his/her contribution when he/she does share.

Our timid person tends to be:

D. PRE-CHRISTIAN

- Love him/her, pray for him/her, call him/her, validate his/her questions 'What a great question!"
- Allow the group to help correct his/her misconceptions as much as possible so that you can help maintain your relationship with him/her as his/her leader.
- When you need to correct say, "You almost have it…" or "That is a helpful insight, but I think the Bible might more accurately communicate that…."
- If you cannot answer his/her question, thank her for asking it and say, "That's a great question. I'll need to do some research and get back to you on that one."
- For the prayer time remind them:
    a. There is NO PRESSURE to pray. "You can pray when you feel ready."

Our pre-Christian or seeker is:

Group discussion follow-up skills when answers to questions are given

A. Skills that build confidence and trust in you as a leader.	
Attending	Focus physically and emotionally on the person speaking. Be devoted in love to that individual.
Affirmation	Compliment answers to build confidence in speaking: - "I'm glad you brought that up, I hadn't thought of that." - "Excellent answer."
Paraphrasing	Saying back to the group member what you think is being said. This checks accuracy and lets the group know you are listening. - "I understand you to say … Is that right?"
Tracking	Keep the group from getting off track and/or from allowing one person to do all the talking. - " I feel we are drifting from the subject." - "Thanks, Jim, for your insights. What do the rest of you think?"
Hanging loose	Exhibit openness to each person and her opinions. Learn to be shock proof. Don't be overly reactive when someone says something that disturbs you.

B. Skills that assist the group member to say what is on his/her mind	
Adding	Drawing more comments from the speaker. - What else did you notice?" - "Could you expand on that?"
Clarifying	Making the meaning clearer - "I'm not sure what you mean by that. Do you mean …? - "Could you rephrase that for me?"
Justifying	Be non-threatening when asking justifying questions - "How do you support your conclusion?" - "Where do you find that in the passage?"

Adapted from Tom Erickson's *Small Group Leadership Training Manual*

C. Skills that involve group members in the discussion	

Extending	Building on line of thought or including others, especially non-talkers. Avoid pressuring shy people.
	  - "Have we left anything out?"
	  - "Does anyone else have something to add?"

Re-directing	Questions to the leader could be re-directed to others.
	  - "I would be interested in what Jane has to say about that. Jane, what do you think?"
	  or "Good question! How would some of the rest of you answer that?"

Discussion Flow

Adapted from Tom Erickson's Small Group Leadership Training Manual

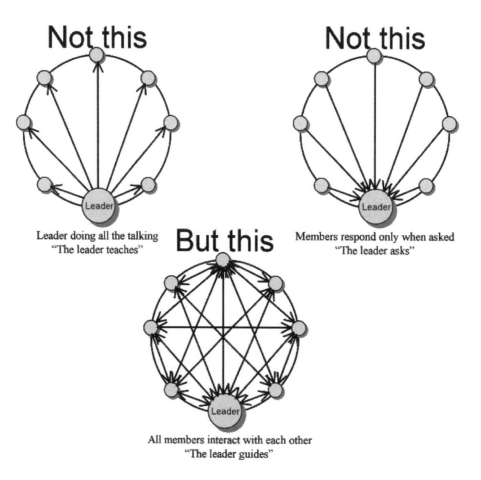

Not this
Leader doing all the talking
"The leader teaches"

Not this
Members respond only when asked
"The leader asks"

But this
All members interact with each other
"The leader guides"

LEARNING CURVES

THE LEARNING CURVE EFFECT

The learning curve effect states that the more times a task has been performed, the less time will be required on each subsequent iteration.

THE EXPERIENCE CURVE EFFECT

The experience curve effect is broader in scope than the learning curve effect encompassing far more than just labor time. It states that the more often a task is performed the lower will be the cost of doing it. The task can be the production of any good or service.

What are the implications of the above effects?

Where are you on your learning curve?

What experience are you bringing to the process?

- o Life experience
- o Previous Bible study experience
- o Previous leadership experience
- o Previous Bible study leadership experience

SMALL GROUP DYNAMICS
TIMING ISSUES

Tips for
STARTING &
ENDING
Meetings
ON TIME

135

All This and On-Time to Worship Too?
OR
All This and Home in Bed by 9:30 Too?

The age old question for a small group leader is always, how can I get through this lesson AND take prayer requests AND pray together AND be on time for worship OR be at home in bed by 9:30?

Here are a few suggestions that others have found helpful:

1. **Don't try to read every Scripture**. Read only a few each week, those that will bring the most "bang for the buck," as the old saying goes. Read ones that tend to speak to the heart of the issue. Decide ahead of time which ones you will read, so you aren't trying to decide "on the spot." Read only a handful each week.

2. **Don't try to answer every question.** Decide ahead of time which questions you will ask. Decisions made "on the spot" are always slower decisions for all of us (and therefore waste precious time) and usually aren't as full of good wisdom about the overall feel of the lesson.

3. **When dealing with questions that are in chart form or have several Scriptures**, ask, "What verse(s) on this chart or in this question spoke to you the most this week? Could you share with us why? Or which Scripture taught you the most about God's definition of "peace?"

4. **Put the time in your margin for each question** you intent to ask (9:40, 9:50, etc.) Don't mark a question as 5 minutes, 3 minutes, etc. It is much easier to know if you are on time or behind if you mark the questions with the time you hope to start the question.

5. **To aid you in timing, place a watch or cell phone with clock on the table** so you do not have to keep checking the wall or your wrist for the time. Use a comment like, Men and women, we're a bit behind on time, so to catch up I would like us to jump over to question # 7.

6. **Use index cards for the recording and reading of prayer requests**. If your group is getting long-winded, ask them to please read their requests without commentary.

7. It can be helpful to **read the prayer requests from the index cards** at the beginning of your class (**without comment or with little comment**) and then pray for the last 5-7 minutes of your class. Your worship leaders (a.m. WOW) can then be present for the sharing of prayer requests even if they miss the prayer time. Realize that worship leaders could go a whole year and never hear a prayer request if requests are always given at the end of your class.

8. **To facilitate sign-ups in your baskets, ask your connection coordinators to be responsible for sending sign-up sheets around your table/group**. Try not to lose too much time discussing the "basket" items. The main goal is to get the sign-up sheet or the envelopes quickly identified and then sent around the room. Do NOT wait to start the class until the sheet has made its way around the table. Start teaching or taking prayer requests WHILE the sheets etc. are being passed. In this day of multi-tasking, your group can DO IT!

9. **Rotate what you skimp on....**one week the taking of prayer requests (read without comment), the next week a shorter prayer time, the next less time on application question, etc. Variety is the spice of life. Decide ahead of time where you will skimp!

10. **Pray for the Spirit's good use of time**. Let His peace lead you and don't hesitate to move on when you sense His nudge.

Tips for leading through a long lesson:

1. Pace yourself so you can cover SOME of EACH day.

2. Don't try to answer every question or read every Scripture. Decide ahead of time which questions you will ask and which Scriptures you will read. BE PURPOSEFUL AND SELECTIVE. Don't try to make decisions on the spot. Use your LESSON REVIEW as your guide.

3. Discern the BIG PICTURE of the lesson and be prepared to summarize BIG PICTURE points when needed. To save time, summarize a few key questions, each as a one-minute lecture, without asking for discussion. Keep your summaries short so participants can capture the BIG PICTURE point of the question you are summarizing and not get caught in the details. Don't try to summarize every question you skip. Be SELECTIVE and PURPOSEFUL!

4. Use the Leader's Sheet to help guide you in the selection of questions. The questions have been selected to help you concentrate on the most important questions to aid the in a clear understanding of the text *and* its application to our everyday lives.

5. Choose a good balance of thinking/feeling questions, with a stronger emphasis on thinking questions. The feeling questions will promote personal discussion but will also take much longer to answer. Be SELECTIVE and PURPOSEFUL!

6. Decide ahead of time what statements may be helpful to use at key points of transition. Write these transitional or summary statements into your lesson so they are at the tip of your tongue, when needed.

7. Place the time in the margin (10:05, 10:10) so you can quickly glance at your watch to help you stay on track.

8. In case you get behind on your time, decide prior to class which questions or day(s) you will drop to get caught up. Remember that getting to worship on time is more important than finishing the lesson, so that each small group participant experiences all the blessings God has in mind for them for the morning.

9. Major on the JUST A MOMENT questions, in that everyone should have had time to answer those. DIGGING DEEPER questions are good questions to summarize, but don't feel you have to summarize all of them. Be SELECTIVE and PURPOSEFUL!

10. Pray, pray, pray and let the Holy Spirit lead you! He promises to empower you for the work to which He has called you. And remember, YOU are on a LEARNING CURVE! So give yourself permission to not have to do it perfectly!!! We will as well! We are truly full of grace at Grace Baptist Church!

ADDITIONAL OPTIONS FOR TRAINING IN LEADERSHIP SKILLS

FIVE LEVELS OF LEADERSHIP BY JOHN MAXWELL

5

PERSONHOOD
Respect

People follow because of who you are and what you represent.

NOTE: This step is reserved for leaders who have spent years growing people & organizations. Few make it. Those who do are bigger than life.

PEOPLE DEVELOPMENT

Reproduction

People follow because of what you have done for them.

NOTE: This is where long-range growth occurs. Your commitment to developing leaders will ensure ongoing growth to the organization and to people. Do whatever you can to achieve and stay on this level.

3

PRODUCTION

Results

People follow because of what you have done for the organization.

NOTE: This is where success is sensed by most people. They like you and what you are doing. Problems are fixed with very little effort because of momentum.

2

PERMISSION

Relationships
People follow because they want to.

NOTE: People will follow you beyond your stated authority. This level allows work to be fun. Caution: Staying too long on this level without rising will cause highly motivated people to become restless.

1

POSITION

Rights

People follow because they have to.

NOTE: Your influence will not extend beyond the lines of your job description. This longer you stay here, the higher the turnover and the lower the morale.

143

144

CLIMBING THE STEPS OF LEADERSHIP
Leadership is influence, nothing more, nothing less.

The higher you go,
the longer it takes.

Each time there is a change in your job or you join a new circle of friends, you start on the lowest level and begin to work yourself up the steps.

Jesus' Ministry: It is estimated that Jesus was in ministry for about a year before He even called the disciples. (Winter of '27 AD Jesus begins public ministry. Winter of '28 AD Jesus chooses the 12 disciples, although some had already been following Him.)

Your Ministry: It takes time to help others feel a part of any group. It doesn't happen overnight.

The higher you go,
the higher the level of commitment.

This increase in commitment is a two-way-street. Greater commitment is demanded not only from you but also from the other individuals involved. When either the leader or the follower is unwilling to make the sacrifices a new level demands, influence will begin to decrease.

Jesus' Ministry: Mk. 3:13-19 – choosing of the 12 disciples. Jn. 6:60-69 – disciples continue to follow when others fall away.

Your Ministry: Some may fall away when the level of commitment gets higher.

The higher you go,
the easier it is to lead.

Notice the progression from level two through level four. The focus goes from liking you to liking what you do for the common interest of all concerned to liking what you do for them personally x. Each level climbed by the leader and the followers adds another reason why people will want to follow.

Jesus' Ministry: Mk. 6:7-13 – Christ drawing out the gifts of the disciples by sending them out 2 by 2.

Your Ministry: your personal caring (level 2) to excellent discussion (level 3) to helping them grow as moms, aunts, friends, etc. or in development of their own gifts and growth in their own ministry (level 4)

The higher you go,
the greater the growth.

Growth can only occur when effective change takes place. Change will become easier as you climb the levels of leadership. As you rise, other people will allow and even assist you in making needed changes.

Jesus' Ministry: Acts 1:5-8 - YOU shall be my witnesses in Jerusalem, Judea, Samaria and the ends of the earth. Disciples moving out in ministry in the name of Jesus.

Your Ministry: Others in your group will help to bring about a greater cohesiveness. It all won't depend on your personal ministry but on their ministry to one another.

You never leave the base level.

Each level stands upon the previous one and will crumble if the lower level is neglected. For example, if you move from a permission (relationships) level to a production (results) level and stop caring for the people who are following you and helping you produce, they might begin to develop a feeling of being used. As you move up in the levels, the deeper and more solid your leadership will be with a person or group of people.

Jesus' Ministry: Mark 1:29-31 - Jesus heals Peter's mother-in-law. Luke 8:22-25 - Jesus caring for the disciples in the storm. Mark 3:7 - Jesus withdrew with his disciples to the lake. Mark 6:45-52 – Jesus walks on the water to the disciples. stretching their personal faith.

Your Ministry: Your continued personal caring for individuals in the group will be essential for your leadership to be respected and responded to.

For your leadership to remain effective, it is essential that you take the other influencers within the group with you to the higher levels.

The collective influence of you and the other leaders will bring the rest along. If this does not happen, divided interest and loyalty will occur within the group.

Jesus' Ministry: Jesus' focus on the 3 influencers – Peter, James and John. Mark 9:2-13 (Mount of Transfiguration), Luke 8:49-56 (Jesus heals 12 year old girl), Luke 22:29-46 (Jesus prays in the garden).

Your Ministry: Who are the influencers in your group? In what ways can they help you influence the rest of the group?

146

DISCUSS, DON'T DOMINATE!

By Terrell Clemmons from
"Discipleship Journal"

An effective small group leader directs without dominating. Here are some guidelines for facilitating small group discussion:

Wait out the silence. After you ask a question, don't rush to rephrase or answer it. Allow group members time to think.

Watch faces. If you see the wheels turning, invite members to think aloud: "Sue, did you have a thought you'd like to share?"

Ask follow-up questions. This draws the speaker out and helps everyone think about the subject more thoroughly. You might ask:
- "What do you mean by that?"
- "In what way?"
- "Why do you think that is?"

Know when to contribute. You don't need to do what your group members have already done. If a member has offered a gentle, appropriate correction to a wrong answer, it's not necessary to add to it. If the group has covered a question well and your answer is the same, go to the next question.

However, if you have a different answer to offer, do so respectfully. "I thought of it from a different angle" and, "We really see this differently, don't we?" are good ways to introduce your idea.

Consult the group. When a member asks you a question, let the group add the input first. Someone else may have an excellent response. You can summarize with your answer afterward if it would help.

Monitor tangents. Decide if a tangent fits the purpose of the group. Allow those that are beneficial, but refocus on a discussion that's gone too far off subject or degenerated into meaningless chatter. Sometimes a knowing smile and a "Getting back to question seven . . ." are sufficient. If your group wants to address a tangential issue in more detail, consider scheduling a separate meeting to examine it.

Affirm members' input without condescending. Don't over-comment. Correct their responses gently when necessary.

Encourage quieter members. Some members are more reluctant to share than others. Consider gentle invitations. "Jan, we'd love to hear from you. Do you have

BEING UNIQUELY YOU!

a. Where do you prefer to **focus your attention**? **The EI Scale**

EXTROVERT (75% of population) versus INTROVERT (25% of population)

Sociability ....Territoriality
Re-energize by being with others....Re-energize alone
Interaction............................. Concentration
External....................................Internal
Breadth....................................Depth
Extensive................................ Intensive
Multiplicity of Relationships......... Limited Relationships
Expenditure of energy.................Conservation of Energies
Interest in external events............Interest in internal reaction

b. How do you take in information? **The SN Scale**

SENSING (75%% of population) versus **N** -INTUITIVE (25% of population)

Experience...............................Hunches
Past.......................................Future
Realistic..................................Speculative
Perspiration............................Inspiration
Actual.....................................Possible
Down-to-earth..........................Head-in-clouds
Utility......................................Fantasy
Fact..Fiction
Practicality...............................Ingenuity
Sensible..................................Imaginative

c. How do you make decisions? **The TF Scale**

THINKING (40% of female population) VS FEELING (60% female population)

Objective..................................Subjective
Principles.................................Values
Policy......................................Social
Criterion..................................Intimacy
........Firmness...............................Persuasion
Impersonal................................Personal
Justice.....................................Humane
Categories................................Harmony
Standards................................Good or bad
Analysis...................................Sympathy
Allocation.................................Devotion

d. How do you orient outer world?**The JP Scale**

JUDGING (50% of population) PERCEIVING (50% of population)

Settled...Pending
Decided......................................Gather more data
Fixed..Flexible
Planned......................................Spontaneous
Thinks and plans ahead...................Works well under pressure
Makes decisions ahead of time... ....Makes decisions at last minute

BEING UNIQUELY YOU!

1. What do I love about my leadership style? What positive benefits can I bring to my group from being "UNIQUELY ME!"

2. Which one or two of my weaknesses do I need to be aware of in order to lead effectively? What can I do to compensate for my weaknesses?

WHAT'S YOUR CONFLICT MANAGEMENT STYLE?

Instructions: Listed below are 15 statements. Each strategy provides a possible strategy for dealing with a conflict. Give each a numerical value **(i.e., 1=Always, 2=Very often, 3=Sometimes, 4= Not very often, 5= Rarely, if ever.)**
Don't answer as you think you should, answer as you actually behave.

_____ a. I argue my case with peers, colleagues and coworkers to demonstrate the merits of the position I take.

_____ b. I try to reach compromises through negotiation.

_____ c. I attempt to meet the expectation of others.

_____ d. I seek to investigate issues with others in order to find solutions that are mutually acceptable.

_____ e. I am firm in resolve when it comes to defending my side of the issue.

_____ f. I try to avoid being singled out, keeping conflict with others to myself.

_____ g. I uphold my solutions to problems.

_____ h. I compromise in order to reach solutions.

_____ i. I trade important information with others so that problems can be solved together.

_____ j. I avoid discussing my differences with others.

_____ k. I try to accommodate the wishes of my peers and colleagues.

_____ l. I seek to bring everyone's concerns out into the open in order to resolve disputes in the best possible way.

_____ m. I put forward middle positions in efforts to break deadlocks.

_____ n. I accept the recommendations of colleagues, peers, and coworkers.

_____ o. I avoid hard feelings by keeping my disagreements with others to myself.

Scoring: The 15 statements you just read are listed below under five categories. Each category contains the letters of three statements. Record the number you placed next to each statement. Calculate the total under each category.

151

Style				Total
Competing/Forcing Shark	a. _____	e._____	g. _____	
Collaborating Owl	d. _____	i. _____	l. _____	
Avoiding Turtle	f. _____	j. _____	o. _____	
Accommodating Teddy Bear	c._____	k. _____	n. _____	
Compromising Fox	b. _____	h. _____	m. _____	

Results:

My dominant style is _____ (Your **LOWEST** score)

My back-up style is _____ (Your second Lowest score)

Source: Mastering Human Relations, 3rd Ed. by A. Falikowski 2002 Pearson Education
http://www.pearsoned.ca

Conflict Management Styles

The Competing Shark

Jesus, our Example

Sharks use a forcing or competing conflict management style

Sharks are highly goal-oriented

Relationships take on a lower priority

Sharks do not hesitate to use aggressive behavior to resolve conflicts

Sharks can be autocratic, authoritative, and uncooperative; threatening and intimidating

Sharks have a need to win; therefore others must lose, creating win-lose situations

Advantage: If the shark's decision is correct, a better decision without compromise can result

Disadvantage: May breed hostility and resentment toward the person using it

Appropriate times to use a Shark style:
- when conflict involves personal differences that are difficult to change
- when fostering intimate or supportive relationships is not critical
- when others are likely to take advantage of noncompetitive behavior
- when conflict resolution is urgent; when decision is vital in crisis
- when unpopular decisions need to be implemented
•

Competing Skills
- Arguing or debating
- Using rank or influence
- Asserting your opinions and feelings
- Standing your ground
- Stating your position clearly

Mark 8:31-33
Jesus Rebukes Peter
Get you behind me, Satan.

Your Notes:

The Avoiding Turtle

Turtles adopt an avoiding or withdrawing conflict management style

Turtles would rather hide and ignore conflict than resolve it; this leads them uncooperative and unassertive

Turtles tend to give up personal goals and display passive behavior creating lose-lose situations

Advantage: may help to maintain relationships that would be hurt by conflict resolution

Disadvantage: Conflicts remain unresolved, overuse of the style leads to others walking over them

Appropriate times to use a Turtle Style:
- when the stakes are not high or issue is trivial
- when confrontation will hurt a working relationship
- when there is little chance of satisfying your wants
- when disruption outweighs benefit of conflict resolution
- when gathering information is more important than an immediate decision
- when others can more effectively resolve the conflict
- when time constraints demand a delay

Avoiding Skills
- Ability to withdraw • Ability to sidestep issues
- Ability to leave things unresolved • Sense of timing for collaboration, some people will profess that the collaboration mode is always the best conflict mode to use.

Jesus, our Example

Matt. 27:12-26
Jesus Before Pilate
Then Pilate asked him, "Don't you hear the testimony they are bringing against you?" But Jesus made no reply, not even to a single charge, to the great amazement of the governor.

Your Notes:

The Accommodating Teddy Bear

Teddy bears use a smoothing or accommodating conflict management style with emphasis on human relationships

Teddy bears ignore their own goals and resolve conflict by giving into others; unassertive and cooperative creating a win-lose (bear is loser) situation

Advantage: Accommodating maintains relationships

Disadvantage: Giving in may not be productive, bear may be taken advantage of

Appropriate times to use a Teddy Bear Style
- when maintaining the relationship outweighs other considerations
- when suggestions/changes are not important to the accommodator
- when minimizing losses in situations where outmatched or losing
- when time is limited or when harmony and stability are valued

Accommodating Skills
- Forgetting your desires
- Selflessness
- Ability to yield
- Obeying orders

Mark 14:32-35
Jesus in the Garden
Father, take this cup from me. Yet not what I will, but your will be done.

Your Notes:

The Compromising Fox

Foxes use a compromising conflict management style; concern is for goals and relationships

Foxes are willing to sacrifice some of their goals while persuading others to give up part of theirs

Compromise is assertive and cooperative-result is either win-lose or lose-lose

Advantage: relationships are maintained and conflicts are removed

Disadvantage: compromise may create less than ideal outcome and game playing can result

Appropriate times to use a Fox Style
- when important/complex issues leave no clear or simple solutions
- when all conflicting people are equal in power and have strong interests in different solutions
- when there are no time restraints

Compromising Skills
- Negotiating
- Finding a middle ground
- Assessing value
- Making concessions

The Collaborating Owl

Owls use a collaborating or problem confronting conflict management style valuing their goals and relationships

Owls view conflicts as problems to be solved finding solutions agreeable to all sides (win-win)

Advantage: both sides get what they want and negative feelings eliminated

Disadvantage: takes a great deal of time and effort

Appropriate times to use an Owl Style
- when maintaining relationships is important
- when time is not a concern
- when peer conflict is involved
- when trying to gain commitment through consensus building
- when learning and trying to merge differing perspectives

Collaboration Skills
- Active listening
- Non-threatening confrontation
- Identifying concerns
- Analyzing input

Jesus, our Example

Matt. 17:24-27
Jesus Pays the Temple Tax
"What do you think Simon? From whom do the kings of the earth collect taxes—from their own sons or from others?" "From others," Peter answered.
Then the sons are exempt. But so that we may not offend them, go to the lake and throw out your line. Take the 1ˢᵗ fish you catch, open its mouth and you will find a four drachmua coin. Take it and give it to them for my tax and yours.

Your Notes:

Mark 6:30-44
Jesus Feeds the 5000
"Send them away."
"You give them something to eat." man's wage."
"How many loaves do you have? Go and see."
Mark 9:33-35
Jesus Answers the Question, "Who is the Greatest?"
"If anyone wants to be first, he must be last and the servant of all."

Your Notes:

IF YOU HAD TO MAKE A CHOICE AS A LEADER, WHICH WOULD YOU DO?

1. Aim to answer every question OR Aim to have a really good discussion of most questions.

2. Call on a quiet member of the group OR Have a quiet member say nothing all morning long

3. Allow a dominant individual to answer most OR Confront the dominant individual
    of the questions   regarding her behavior

4. Allow an upset individual to share his.her heart extensively OR Move the group back
                                                                         to the Bible
                                                                         lesson?

5. Allow an individual who states a biblical inaccuracy to go unchallenged
    OR Challenge the biblical inaccuracy with personal insight
    OR allow the group to address the biblical inaccuracies as much as possible.

GOAL #3: TRAINING OF SMALL GROUP LEADERS

SECTION C:
BIBLICAL SKILLS

BIBLICAL HELPS FOR

OLD TESTAMENT STUDIES

Seven Old Testament Historical Periods

Period 1: Period of Beginnings Genesis 1-11. In the 1st 11 chapters of the Bible, God begins the world. He creates the heavens and the earth, all living creatures, and of course, man and woman.

Period 2: Period of the Patriarchs Genesis 12-50. "Patriarchs" means "fathers." From the people of Adam's race, God chose one man, Abraham, to be the father of many nations. From his seed the Savior of the world, Jesus, would be born. To Abraham God promised land as well as many descendants. Abraham begot Isaac who begot Jacob who begot Joseph (the four patriarchs). From Jacob, who had twelve sons, come the twelve tribes of Israel.

Period 3: The Nation of Israel Exodus, Leviticus, Numbers, Deuteronomy. These twelve tribes grow and become a great nation. They are first slaves in Egypt after Jacob's son Joseph dies. Moses then becomes God's man to lead the Israelites out of slavery into the Promised Land, the land originally promised to Abraham. During this time Moses receives the law and the 10 commandments that the Israelites continually disobeyed. Because of their rebellion, God allows them to wander in the desert for 40 years until a whole generation of Jews dies off.

Period 4: The Occupation Joshua, Judges, Ruth. Moses dies and God raises up Joshua to lead this new generation into the Promised Land to occupy it (thus the period is called the period of occupation). In the process of completing "the occupation," God tells the Israelites to kill off everyone in the land to protect themselves from the temptation to inter-marry and/or worship other gods. They disobey and soon every man is "doing what is right in his own eyes" (Judges 21:25). During this period, the Israelites have God as their king while God raises up judges to settle disputes between the people.

Period 5: The United Kingdom I & II Samuel, I Kings 1-12, I Chronicles, II Chronicles 1-9. The nation of Israel tires of being ruled by judges so they ask God for a king like all the other nations. Saul, David, & Solomon are the three kings that rule when the nation is united.

Period 6: The Divided Kingdom II Kings 13-24, II Chronicles 10-36. The kingdom divides under the leadership of Rehoboam and Jeroboam, Solomon's sons. Ten tribes go to the north (called Israel) and two tribes go to the south (called Judah) and become two separate kingdoms. Each has its own succession of kings that rule and prophets that prophesy.

Period 7: Exile and Restoration Ezra, Nehemiah, Esther. Because of the rebellion of the Jews, God uses other nations to discipline them. Other kingdoms conquer both Judah and Israel. God allows them to be exiled as they suffer the consequences of their sin. Ezra, Nehemiah, and Esther record the history of the exiled Israelites and their beginning return to the Promised Land.

The Remainder of the Old Testament books can be divided into:
- **The Poetic Books:** Job, Psalms, Proverbs, Ecclesiastes, Song of Solomon
- **The Prophetic Books:**
    Major Prophets: Isaiah, Jeremiah, Lamentations, Ezekiel, Daniel
    Minor Prophets: Hosea, Joel, Amos, Obadiah, Jonah, Micah, Nahum, Habakkuk, Zephaniah, Haggai, Zachariah, Malachi

Seven Old Testament Historical Periods

Historical Period	Key Characters	Key Verse	Key Books
I. Beginnings	Adam and Eve Cain and Abel Noah	"In the beginning God created the heavens and the earth." Genesis 1:1	Genesis 1-11
II. Patriarchs	Abraham Isaac Jacob Joseph	"I will make you a great nation and I will bless you . . . all the nations of the earth will be blessed through you." Genesis 12:2,3	Genesis 12-50
III. Nation of Israel	Moses and Aaron	"Now if you obey me fully and keep my Covenant, then out of all nations you will be my treasured possession. Although the whole earth is mine, you will be for me a kingdom of priests and a holy nation." Exodus 19:5-6	Exodus, Leviticus, Deuteronomy
IV. Occupation	Joshua, Gideon Samson, Ruth	"In those days Israel had no king and everyone did what was right in his own eyes." Judges 12:25	Joshua, Judges, Ruth
V. United Kingdom	Samuel Saul David & Jonathan Solomon	"We want a king over us. Then we will be like all the other nations with a king to lead us and go out before us and fight our battles." I Samuel 8:19-20	I & II Samuel I Kings 1-12 I Chronicles II Chronicles 1-9
VI. Divided Kingdom	Jeroboam and Rehoboam Jehoshaphat Hezekiah Elijah Elisha	"The Lord, the God of their fathers, sent word to them through his messengers again and again, because He had pity on His people and on His dwelling place. But they mocked God's messengers, despised his words and scoffed at his prophets until the wrath of the Lord was aroused against his people and there was no remedy." 2 Chronicles 36:15-16	II Chronicles 36:15-16 I Kings 13-22 II Kings II Chronicles 10-36
VII. Exile & Restoration	Daniel Ezra Nehemiah Esther	"I had not told anyone what God had put in the heart to do for Jerusalem." Nehemiah 1:12	Daniel Ezra Nehemiah Esther

What biblical skills can be taught to small group leaders to enhance their own study of the Word?

The following is a list of biblical skills from which you can choose when training small group leaders beyond the kick-off training in September. Each set of skills can be located under Goal #1: Section A of this manual:

1. Observation skills
2. Interpretation skills
3. Correlation skills
4. Application skills
5. Word studies
6. Warning about misinterpreting Scripture/appropriate use of commentaries
7. Warnings about misapplying Scripture/abstraction ladder
8. Structuring

GOAL #3: TRAINING OF SMALL GROUP LEADERS

SECTION D: SHEPHERDING SKILLS

SMALL GROUP DYNAMICS BONDING

Helping Group Members Process Growing Pains

Stage	Formation	Exploration	Transition
# of Meetings per Stage	4 to 6	6 to 8	8 to 10
Member's Questions	Who is in the group? Do I like my group?	Do I fit here? How is our group doing?	Are we really open with each other? Will this group accomplish its mission?
Member's Feelings	Excitement Anticipation Awkwardness	Comfortable Relaxed Open	Tense Anxious Impatient Doubtful
Member's Role	Gather Information about Others	Give Information about others	Provide feedback Express frustration
Leader's Response	Caring Clear Accepting	Affirmation Feedback Warmth Modeling	Confront Encourage Challenge
Leader's Role	Communicate vision Promote sharing	Generate trust Discuss values Facilitate relationships Create covenant	Provide self-disclosure Re-examine covenant Be flexible

SMALL GROUP DYNAMICS

PRAYER TIME

Helping Group Members Grow in Deeper Intimacy in Prayer

A. Help them to understand what prayer is—a conversation with God. Contrast conversational prayer with traditional prayers.

1. Traditional prayer is a monologue; one person prays while others presumably listen.
2. Traditional prayer has fixed patterns of speech and uses outmoded language.
3. Conversational prayer was illustrated by Jesus when He used terms like "Abba Father," the speech of a child to his father.

B. Encourage prayer that includes:

1. **Adoration** – praising God for who He is.
2. **Confession** – admitting our true condition in the sight of God, including general creatureliness as well as particular sins.
3. **Thanksgiving** – expressing gratitude for all that God has done for us and given us.
4. **Supplication** – specific requests for our own needs as well as the needs of others.

Note: Sometimes a biblical passage will naturally focus on just one of these four types of prayer. Beware of the tendency to pray as a group only in terms of supplication.

C. Explain that in conversational prayer, each person should:

1. Speak naturally.
2. Pray audibly.
3. Pray in tune by not prematurely introducing a new subject.
4. Not monopolize the conversation. Take turns, listen, wait.
5. Feel free to speak more than once.
6. Not be afraid of silence.

D. Encourage conversational prayer that is specific and realistic.

1. Prayer arising out of application questions based on the biblical text.
2. Prayer arising from discussion of schedule and relationships.
3. Prayer that stretches their faith.
4. Prayer that alternates between requests for oneself and for others in the group. In "supportive prayer," each person intercedes for the previous person before offering his/her own request.

E. Help those in the group who are reluctant to pray out loud.

1. Help them feel at ease.
   a. Don't force them or embarrass them.
   b. Let them know that others have the same shyness.
2. Design prayer situations that are as simple as possible (e.g. one-word prayers, or sentence prayers).

3. Break up into smaller groups for sharing of prayer requests. Sometimes people feel freer to pray with two or three others than in a group ten or twelve.
4. Lead the group through a step-wise growth process in prayer over several weeks.
    - Week 1 – Leader prays.
    - Week 2 – One-word prayers of thanksgiving.
    - Week 3 – One-word prayers of petition. "Lord I need ... strength, wisdom, love, understanding, forgiveness, patience, help, etc."
    - Week 4 – Each person shares a prayer request, then offers a simple sentence prayer for the person on the right.
    - Week 5 – People pair off for prayer partnerships.
    - Week 6 – Introduce topical prayer, where each prayer builds on the previous one, until the conversation shifts to another topic. People should pray more than once if they wish, but people are encouraged to keep their prayers brief.
    - Week 7 – Continue to practice topical prayer.
5. In your own devotional times, pray for the members of your group in terms of what God desires them to become—free to converse with God in the presence of His people

F. Keep moving toward greater depth of intimacy in prayer.

Five Levels of Communication	Examples from Conversation	Examples from Prayer
Clichés	"How are you doing today?" "Nice weather, isn't it?"	"Bless this food to our bodies and us to Thy service." "Now I lay me down to sleep; I pray the Lord my soul to keep."
Information	"We have two children." "I came right from work, and haven't had dinner."	"Lord, we have come together tonight to study your Word and to pray for one another." "God, we bring to you needs of our members who were sick and unable to come tonight."
Ideas and Opinions	"I think that our church has effective training for small group leaders." "Do you believe that suffering builds Christian character?"	"Jesus I believe that you are showing us that it is time for us to invite some more people to our group." "Lord, do you want me to take this new job? Please show me your will."
Feelings and Values	"The members of the group have come to mean a great deal to me." "I desire to make a positive impact for Jesus Christ on my family, and on the people with whom I work."	"Jesus, I love you and I love these brothers and sisters." "God, I so long to see my children solidly established in their faith."
Intimacy and Confession	"I am feeling that God has abandoned me, that He is no longer listening to my prayers, and that He can never forgive me." "I would like you to tell about a special vision that I believe God has for my life."	"Lord, please forgive me for my spiritual coldness and for trying to fool this group about the real spiritual condition of my heart." "Father, if you are willing, take this cup from me; yet not my will but yours be done.

ADDITIONAL OPTIONS FOR TRAINING IN SHEPHERDING SKILLS

Helping Group Members Process Growing Pains

Stage	Formation	Exploration	Transition
# of Meetings per Stage	4 to 6	6 to 8	8 to 10
Member's Questions	Who is in the group? Do I like my group?	Do I fit here? How is our group doing?	Are we really open with each other? Will this group accomplish its mission?
Member's Feelings	Excitement Anticipation Awkwardness	Comfortable Relaxed Open	Tense Anxious Impatient Doubtful
Member's Role	Gather Information about Others	Give Information about others	Provide feedback Express frustration
Leader's Response	Caring Clear Accepting	Affirmation Feedback Warmth Modeling	Confront Encourage Challenge
Leader's Role	Communicate vision Promote sharing	Generate trust Discuss values Facilitate relationships Create covenant	Provide self-disclosure Re-examine covenant Be flexible

Reflections on our Group's Progress toward Bonding & Intimacy
Church Value: Authentic Community

1. Review "Helping Group Members Process Growing Pains"(page 171)

a. Determine present stage

b. Reflect on group member's feelings

c. Review leader's role and response. How are we doing as leaders?

d. Reflect on content and style of communication

What have we done well? What could we do differently?

What one or two steps can we take to help our group members process our growing pains?

2. Review "Helping Group Members Grow in Deeper Intimacy in Prayer" (pages 167-168)

a. Which levels of communication is the group using with each other most frequently?

b. In promoting intimacy, what have we done well?

c. What one or two steps could we take to promote greater intimacy in our small group? Be specific. If possible, create measurable goals.

3. **Reflect on EACH group member's bonding with other group members.**
   Understanding that individuals attend Bible studies to 1) grow in Bible study 2) grow in Christ-centered friendships, how are EACH of our participants doing in connecting with other women in our group?

   1)

   2)

   3)

   4)

   5)

   6)

   7)

   8)

   9)

   10)

   11)

   12)

   Which individuals are the least connected? List them.

181

Shepherding the flock

From the following Scriptures, what do you learn about how a shepherd is to shepherd the sheep? What insight can you glean from each about how you can shepherd the people in your small group?

Scriptural Description of Shepherd	Implications for Shepherding your Flock
Jn. 10:2 Enters by the gate (as compared with thief or robber climbing in by some other way)	
Jn. 10:3 Sheep listen to the shepherd's voice	
Jn. 10: 3 He calls his own sheep by name and leads them out.	
Jn. 10:4 Sheep follow him because they know his voice	
Jn. 10:5 Sheep never follow a stranger; in fact, they will run away from him because they do not recognize a stranger's voice.	
Jn. 10:11 The Good Shepherd lays down his life for the sheep.	
Ps. 23:1 With the Lord as Shepherd, the sheep are never in want.	
Ps. 23:2 The Shepherd makes the sheep lie down in green pastures.	
Ps. 23:2 The Shepherd leads the sheep beside quiet waters and restores his/her soul.	
Ps. 23:3 The Shepherd guides the sheep in paths of righteousness for His name's sake	
Ps. 23:4 The Shepherd walks through the valley of the shadow of death with the sheep	
Ps. 23:4 The Shepherd's rod (of correction) and staff (of direction) comfort the sheep.	
1 Pet. 5:2 Shepherd God's flock under your care, serving as overseers—not because you must, but because you are willing as God wants you to be.	

Telephone Role Plays
1. Role play calling a group member who is struggling with the length of her lesson and tempted to drop out of Bible study or even has not been coming recently. Remember to shepherd them first, before dealing with the real issue.

2. Role play calling a group member whom you would like to encourage to help you in shepherding another individual in your group.

THE ART OF UNDERSTANDING COMMUNICATION BREAKDOWN
LEARNING TO ACCURATELY COMMUNICATE MY HEART & HEAR THE HEART
OF SOMEONE ELSE

VOICE/BODY
LANGUAGE OF
OF
COMMUNICATOR

EARS
OF
LISTENER

HEART OF
COMMUNICATOR

HEART OF
LISTENER

There are four places where communication can break down between two people:

1) At the Heart of the Communicator

2) The Voice/Body Language of the Communicator

3) The Ears of the Listener

4) The Heart of the Communicator

b) After clarifying what they were trying to say, suggest:
• It is so helpful to hear your heart and what you were trying to say. Perhaps I am not the only one that jumped to wrong conclusions. May I suggest that you say …
do… it a little differently next time so that others might not be misperceiving you as I was? It would help me if you would say . . .? Does that make sense to you?

2. If I am the communicator, what can I do to make sure I am accurately communicating my heart?
a) Ask for feedback.
• How do you think the time went today?
• Do you have any suggestions for me?
• What could I do differently to communicate my heart more accurately?
• Don't shoot the messenger! Be grateful someone loves you enough to hear how you are coming across!

b) Be aware of hiding behind a mask:

> Definition of Mask:
>
> What we know about ourselves that is not known to others.

c) Be aware and ask for help with your blind spots.

> Definition of Blind Spot:
>
> What others know about us that is not personally known to us.

What types of blind spots might we have that could affect our teaching ?

WHETHER YOU ARE THE LISTENER OR THE COMMUNICATOR, BE AWARE THAT COMMUNICATION IS HARD WORK AND THAT IT IS VERY EASY TO MISUNDERSTAND ONE ANOTHER. THE GOAL IS TO COMMUNICATE HEART TO HEART. DON'T ASSUME SOMEONE ELSE'S HEART WITHOUT TAKING THE TIME TO TRULY HEAR THEIR HEART.

SHEPHERDING IN A CRISIS

A Shepherd will stop the bleeding before she/he gives the vitamins. Just as a paramedic first looks at the source of the bleeding, we should focus first on the injury. A patient who is bleeding probably cannot receive instruction on how the accident might have been prevented. What the patient needs at that point is emergency care from someone who understands what is needed to stop the bleeding and what the "normal" symptoms of his specific injury. **Once the initial source of bleeding is discovered and addressed, then more long term and even preventative instruction can be received from the patient's established health care provider.**

Too often the Body of Christ begins with preventative instruction, then long-term directives. The woman is told to memorize Scripture and pray more. This is valuable and needful instruction, but it is not timely when the patient is bleeding emotionally, panic-stricken, or confused. In essence, women are often told, "Just get over it! Stop the tears and just move on... This isn't that bad.

Effective pastoral care to reverses the order of procedure. It focuses first on the emotional pain and how people process emotional pain. Effective pastoral carerecognizes that it is healthy to feel the pain. Crying is cathartic. It is an essential step toward healing.

Then it gives attention to the issues that cause pain. (Quotes taken from *Shepherding a Woman's Heart* by Beverly Hislop.)

> Christ's Examples of STOP THE BLEEDING FIRST:
> 1. Mark 2/Healing of Paralytic - dealt with his physical need first, then his need for forgiveness of sin
> 2. Mary at Tomb of Lazarus - wept with her first but real goal was for her to believe. Jn. 11:14, 20, 35
> 3. Martha at Tomb of Lazarus - dealt with her anger first but real goal was for her to believe Jn. 11:21, 23 **Martha in FIGHT MODE.**
> 4. Mary anointing Jesus for burial - received her expression of love for his burial/she was "tending," and Christ received it. **Mary in FRIGHT MODE**—chose to tend. Jn 12:3
>
> Spirit's Ministry to Elijah to STOP THE BLEEDING FIRST:
> 1. Elijah wanting to die Angel feeds him and helps him rest first. "Get up and eat. The journey is too long for you." "Go back the way you came." Good example of God's mercy to give him energy for a journey he was never suppose to take **Elijah in FLIGHT MODE! Angel met him where he was and then gave him orders to go to Damascus and anoint Hezael** 1 Kings 19:5-6, 8:15

When to Refer:
1) When emotional fusion with client, not intimacy, is happening for you
2) When the issue feels beyond your areas of expertise—
   - eating disorders
   - deep depression
   - suicide
   - addictions - (resulting from hiding from love- issues with lack of bonding)

However, please be open to reading/learning about specific issues. God may call you to develop an area of expertise so that you can be of help to someone else.

3) State a clear boundary: "I can support you, but I cannot be your only support. If you want support from me, I need for you to find 3 other healthy people who also are willing to support

Pat Schwiebert, RN
Grief Watch

What not to say to a grieving person

- Snap out of it
- It wasn't meant to be
- You must be strong
- She lived a good life
- You must move on
- God will never give you more than you can handle
- I understand
- Be thankful you have other children
- It's over with. Let's not deal with it
- Get a hold of yourself
- Keep a stiff upper lip
- Pull yourself together
- Be strong for the children
- Get back on the horse again
- It was God's will
- You can always have other children
- You're young
- Maybe God is trying to teach you a lesson
- Others have it worse than you
- What did you do wrong?
- He wouldn't have been healthy
- It is just nature's way of dealing with a problem

Helpful things to say to a grieving person

- I'm so sorry to hear about your loss
- I can't imagine what you are going through. It must be unbearable.
- Sit down and tell me all about it.
- I don't know what to say, but I'll be glad to listen.
- How are you really feeling?
- What can I do to help?

(if you are caring for someone from a different culture ask "what would be happening if this situation occurred in your culture…?"

GOAL #4: TRAINING OF CURRICULUM WRITING TEAMS

Goal #4: Learn to **train curriculum-writing teams** to create materials that are appropriate for neighborhood and/or church-based Bible studies.

BENEFITS OF TRAINING A CURRICULUM WRITING TEAM

1. **A team brings its collective experience to the writing process**, both biblically and experientially.

2. **The workload can be divided among team members**. No one individual carries too heavy a workload, bears the burden of criticism or even the temptation toward self-glory. Each team member can write a lesson and edit one or two other lessons.

3. After lessons have been assigned and written, to complete the task **team members could function in their areas of giftedness.** Some may be good at layout while others great at editing. Some may shine in the writing of introductions or in the rewriting of excellent application questions. Others may be great at publicizing the start of the new study or prefer to help train the small group leaders.

4. **Team members will grow in depth in their study of God's Word and their desire to teach it to others**. They will also grow in their confidence in handling the Word of God accurately without having to get a seminary degree!

5. **The workbook can be created with the correct number of lessons, the right amount of homework, and the best balance of thinking versus feeling questions.**

6. **The topic or biblical passages can be the primary focus in choosing what will be studied for the year, not finding a workbook that has all the correct criteria for good workbooks,** regardless of the topic or biblical book being studied. Good workbooks geared to the target groups' needs are really hard to find.

7. **The bonding of the team is incredible.** There is nothing more satisfying than creating something for the Lord and His people that has long-lasting impact.

8. **The team concept can be reproduced in other churches if team members are called to a new city or a new church.**

9. **The longer a Bible Study exists, the more difficult it is to find good curriculum,** because the best on the market has already been used in prior years. A curriculum writing team can eliminate or cut down on the endless search for excellent Bible study curriculum.

10. Since most published curriculum are required to have little or no homework, **it is particularly difficult to find good curriculum that requires homework,** if that is the goal of your target group. A team can create curriculum with the desired amount of homework.

11. **A team approach will protect from burnout for an individual curriculum writer.** When burnout or moving away occurs, the Bible study is left wanting. If a team of writers is in place, new team members can be added yearly to replace those who move away or need a break.

Creating a Five-Day Lesson with Day Titles

Many Bible studies are written as five-day curricula. If we revisit the questions, "what is the **target on the wall**" or "**what kind of individual are we trying to produce**," it seems appropriate that we consider her to be an individual who is in God's Word on a daily basis. Therefore a Bible study workbook that challenges its students to study five days a week will adequately aim to meet this goal, thus hitting the desired target.

To create a five-day lesson, begin by writing day-titles aimed at creating life-transforming Bible study curriculum. The following principles are helpful in creating a workbook with lessons and day titles that focus on transforming a woman's life.

1. After studying the book of the Bible or chapter(s) to be included in the workbook, divide the book or biblical chapters into the number of desired lessons. Create lesson divisions at natural breaks in the flow of the book of the Bible or biblical chapters to be included in the workbook.

2. Create lesson titles for each lesson, stating each title in terms of personal application to the Bible student. Below are examples of Lesson Titles for "Experiencing God in the Psalms," a nine week study focused on nine types of Psalms.

Lesson One (Ps. 8, 19, 29, 139)
Marveling at God's Creation

Lesson Two (Ps. 131, 23, 8, 3, 46)
Resting in God's Care

Lesson Three (Ps. 27, 42, 43, 63)
Thirsting After God in Times of Stress

Lesson Four (Ps. 1, 51, 73, 18, 90)
Living Out the Psalms' Wisdom

Lesson Five (Ps. 120-134)
Ascending in Praise through the
Pilgrim Psalms

Lesson Six (Ps.103, 107, 136, 116, 92)
Increasing in Contentment through
Thanksgiving

Lesson Seven (Ps. 55, 137, 18, 62)
Being Real in Victory and Defeat

Lesson Eight (Ps. 45, 22, 2, 110)
Deepening in Love for the Messiah

Lesson Nine (Ps. 40, 71, 78, 92, 96)
Declaring God's Glory

3. Now break down the Scripture for each lesson into five sections, one for each day the student will study.

4. Finally, create day-titles using the same principle utilized for creating the lesson titles. Each day-title should be stated as a personal application to the Bible student. See examples below.

Day One: Psalm 8
Humbled by God's Majestic Creation

Day Two: Psalm 19
Experiencing a Heart Change as a Result
of God's Spoken and Silent Revelations

Day Three: Psalm 29
Listening to God's Voice in Creation

Day Four: Psalm 129
Giving Glory to God for His Kingship Over
Creation

Day Five: Psalm 139
Praising the Creator and Searcher of My
Inmost Soul

CURRICULUM WRITING TEAM CONTRACT

Decisions to be Made:

1. Content of Workbook (book of Bible, topical study, number of lessons, target group)

2. Process of recruitment of curriculum writing team

3. Dates to meet (when and how often)

4. Publication Deadline

5. Strategy for Training of Curriculum Writing Team

   Which documents for teaching?

   How many training sessions prior to writing questions?

6. Due Dates for Drafts:

   First Rough Draft Due:

   Second Rough Draft Due:

   Final Drafts Due:

7. Lesson Strategy (number of questions per lesson? introductions? study notes?, etc.)

8. Formatting Strategy

9. Editing Strategy

Curriculum Writing Team Contract (page 2)

Book Study Title: _____

Chapter Divisions/ Application-Oriented Chapter Titles	Curriculum Writer:

Topical Study Title: _____

Chapter Divisions/ Application-Oriented Chapter Titles	Curriculum Writer:

CURRICULUM WRITING TEAM TRAINING MANUAL

Instructions for Curriculum Writing Team Production Schedule

The following pages contain a template for a curriculum writing team manual. Everything needed for training a curriculum writing team of your own has been included. A five-day production schedule for the team is provided, from day one when the team is given initial curriculum writing training to day five when final drafts of lessons are due and the team process is reviewed and evaluated.

This manual may be used in part or in whole by your church. Please feel free to adapt or modify this process as needed, respecting the copyrights. The author requests that even if you modify this manual, you do not attempt to get your manual published.

The five-day production schedule requires a number of weeks in between the five sessions. The following time sequence and spread of weeks between sessions is highly recommended. The time sequence respects school schedules so that curriculum writing team moms of school-aged children can complete their work by early June in preparation for summer vacation with their children.

DAY ONE	EARLY TO MID FEBRUARY
DAY TWO	EARLY APRIL
DAY THREE	EARLY MAY (one full month is needed between days 2 and 3 for the writing of the lesson)
DAY FOUR	LATE MAY
DAY FIVE	EARLY JUNE

Depending on the level of inductive Bible study skills of your curriculum writing team, you may need to spilt DAY ONE into two days of training. If this be the case, I recommend that your team meet in January to learn basic inductive Bible study skills and in February to learn to write flow questions.

After the curriculum writing team has finished their work, the editing team begins the editing process. I recommend 2-3 women on the editing team. All lessons should be reviewed by all editors who then meet to coordinate their efforts. For maximum productivity, the editing team should aim to edit no more than three lessons at any one sitting. Pictures should be added at this point by one person on the editing team.

After the editing team has completed its work, one final edit may need to be made by a fine-line editor who checks for grammar and punctuation only.

BIBLE STUDY CURRICULUM WRITING TEAM MANUAL
TABLE OF CONTENTS

Instructions to the Trainer of the Curriculum Writing Team

Five Day Lesson Plans (February through early June)

Dear Curriculum Team Trainer,

You are about to venture into the exciting process of drawing out the gifts and talents of the individuals in your church to help create a Bible study workbook that will best meet the needs of those attending your Bible study. This training manual supplies you with all that is needed for the training process. Please read through it carefully yourself, completing all the exercises as if you were a student in your own classroom. You cannot train someone else to do what you haven't mastered yourself.

Many of the skills given in this workbook are probably not new to you, but simply a review of Bible study skills you have learned in other settings. Depending on your experience in writing questions for curriculum, learning to write good questions may be review for you as well. Once you have grasped the basic principles of good Bible study skills and the skills of writing good questions, you are ready to choose and train your team.

From years of experience in working with a curriculum writing team, I highly recommend that each five-day lesson be written by one writer and then reviewed by one helper. Please do not have two individuals try to write the same lesson by dividing up the days. Our team has discovered that the change in writing style between the two writers is evident, creating much added and unnecessary work for the editing team to try to fuse the two writing styles.

I recommend therefore, that your writing team consist of one writer for each lesson and one helper. If you have eight lessons, for example, you will need sixteen women on your team. My recommendation is not to try to write curricula for your entire Bible study year. Start your team small the first year on a shorter writing project and then add members to the team in the coming years for longer projects as your team gains experience.

You may find that the introduction for each lesson takes a different set of writing skills. We have found individuals who love to write our introductions. We look for individuals with strong writing gifts that can write a one page introduction geared to engage the Bible study participant to feel involved in the lesson at the feeling level before she even opens her Bible to begin the thinking process. A good number of our lesson writers feel confident in writing their own introductions, but a good number do not. We have one writer who takes on writing the introductions for those writers who would prefer someone else do that particular creative writing project for her. The team approach allows for team members to bring to the project the gifts God has given each individual, helping all to feel successful as a result.

Prior to the first meeting of your team, lesson titles and day titles will need to be written by you or someone on your team who has BIG PICTURE skills and understands how to create titles that are application oriented. The following page of this manual gives helpful hints for creating appropriate lesson and day titles.

The following website contains examples of Bible study workbooks written with these principles in mind. Please refer to them as part of your own learning curve.
Better Together.
http://www.westernseminary.edu/Women/RESOURCES/BS_Curriculum/Topical/Topical_studies.htm

The Book of Mark
http://www.westernseminary.edu/Women/RESOURCES/BS_Curriculum/Book/Book_studies.NT.htm

May the Lord bless you as you endeavor to trust God for an exciting writing project produced through a team approach for the glory of God.

With great anticipation of your success for Christ's kingdom,
Phyllis Bennett

Creating a Five-Day Lesson with Day Titles

Many studies are written as five-day curricula. If we revisit the question, "what is the target on the wall" *or"* what kind of woman are we trying to produce," it seems appropriate that we consider him/her to be an individual who is in God's Word on a daily basis. Therefore a Bible study workbook that challenges its students to study five days a week will adequately aim to meet this goal, thus hitting the desired target.

To create a five-day lesson, begin by writing day-titles aimed at creating life-transforming Bible study curriculum. The following principles are helpful in creating a workbook with lessons and day titles that focus on transforming a woman's life.

1. After studying the book of the Bible or chapter(s) to be included in the workbook, divide the book or biblical chapters into the number of desired lessons. Create lesson divisions at natural breaks in the flow of the book of the Bible or biblical chapters to be included in the workbook.

2. Create lesson titles for each lesson, stating each title in terms of personal application to the Bible student. Below are examples of Lesson Titles for "Experiencing God in the Psalms," a nine week study focused on nine types of Psalms.

Lesson One (Ps. 8, 19, 29, 139)
Marveling at God's Creation

Lesson Two (Ps. 131, 23, 8, 3, 46)
Resting in God's Care

Lesson Three (Ps. 27, 42, 43, 63)
Thirsting After God in Times of Stress

Lesson Four (Ps. 1, 51, 73, 18, 90)
Living Out the Psalms' Wisdom

Lesson Five (Ps. 120-134)
Ascending in Praise through the
Pilgrim Psalms

Lesson Six (Ps.103, 107, 136, 116, 92)
Increasing in Contentment through
Thanksgiving

Lesson Seven (Ps. 55, 137, 18, 62)
Being Real in Victory and Defeat

Lesson Eight (Ps. 45, 22, 2, 110)
Deepening in Love for the Messiah

Lesson Nine (Ps. 40, 71, 78, 92, 96)
Declaring God's Glory

3. Now break down the Scripture for each lesson into five sections, one for each day the student will study.

4. Finally, create day-titles using the same principle utilized for creating the lesson titles. Each day-title should be stated as a personal application to the Bible student. See examples below.

Day One: Psalm 8
Humbled by God's Majestic Creation

Day Two: Psalm 19
Experiencing a Heart Change as a Result
of God's Spoken and Silent Revelations

Day Three: Psalm 29
Listening to God's Voice in Creation

Day Four: Psalm 129
Giving Glory to God for His Kingship Over
Creation

Day Five: Psalm 139
Praising the Creator and Searcher of My
Inmost Soul

Lesson Plan Curriculum Writing Team Day 1
Date:_____

Time Schedule	Lesson Objective	Page #
9:00-9:15 a.m.	**Setting the Stage:** Worship or 5 minute devotional What sounds fun to you about this project? What did you most enjoy about the process last year?	
9:15-9:20 a.m.	**Learning Curves:** Reducing the fear factor by admitting the obvious—we are ALL on a learning curve, no matter how little or how much experience we bring to the process.	8
9:20-9:30 a.m.	**THE WHY:** Why write curriculum? The Target on the Wall	9
9:30-11:20 a.m. 9:30-9:35 a.m. 9:35-10:05 a.m. 10:05-10:20 a.m. 10:20-10:30 a.m. 10:30-11:20 a.m. 11:20-11:30 a.m.	**THE HOW:** Mastering basic tools needed for curriculum writing • **Understanding** the inductive approach to Bible study • **Introducing** the four steps of inductive Bible study process • **Practicing** Inductive Bible study skills (could do as homework if getting behind on time. Could also substitute Scripture worksheet for a short portion of the book of the Bible your curriculum team will focus on) • Break (suggested snacks - yogurt, fruit, breads) • **Learning** to write types of questions necessary for excellent discussion and personal Bible study satisfaction • **Identifying** Good Questions • **Practicing** writing good questions • **Grasping** the Template (PULL OUT AND PUT IN FRONT OF TRAINING MANUAL)	12 13 28 30 36 38 43
11:30-11:35 a.m.	**THE WHAT AND WHO:** • Team Assignments (PULL OUT AND PUT IN FRONT OF TRAINING MANUAL) • This Year's Curriculum	 45 47
11:35-11:40 a.m.	**THE PROCESS:** • Overview of Writing Process (BIG PICTURE LOOK for those who like to know where the train is headed) • Welcome to First Writing Assignment • Instructions for working on your emailed document	 49 54
11:40-11:55 a.m.	**FIRST LOOK AT YOUR LESSON:** • with partner, notice day titles written as applications	
11:55-noon	**HOW ARE YOUR FEELING?** (one word descriptions) Prayers of thanks for a successful launch	

Depending on the experience of your team, you may want to divide Day 1 into 2 training days. If your team has had a good amount of experience in inductive Bible study skills, one day's training may be sufficient. If inductive Bible study skills are new to your team, you may need 2 days to cover this material, one day for Bible study skills and one for learning to write questions.

LEARNING CURVES

THE LEARNING CURVE EFFECT

The learning curve effect states that the more times a task has been performed, the less time will be required on each subsequent iteration.

THE EXPERIENCE CURVE EFFECT

The experience curve effect is broader in scope than the learning curve effect encompassing far more than just labor time. It states that the more often a task is performed the lower will be the cost of doing it. The task can be the production of any good or service.

What implications can be drawn from each of these above effects?

Where are you on your learning curve?

What experience are you bringing to the process?

- ○ Life experience

- ○ Previous writing experience

- ○ Previous curriculum writing experience

- ○ Previous Bible study experience

LIFE TRANSFORMING BIBLE STUDY CURRICULA: IDENTIFYING THE NEED

When choosing or designing Bible study curricula, where do we begin? What is the target on the wall?

- The portion of the B_____we'll study?
- The a_____ and his/her style of writing?
- The amount of h_____we're willing to do?
- The g_____design and the cover?
- The t_____?
- Strong on p_____ reflection ? Or h_____knowledge? knowledge?

Or do we begin with. . .
What kind of people are we called of God to produce? Scripture gives us these insights:

> Psalms 1:1-3 His/her delight is in the law of the Lord and on His law he/she meditates day and night. He/she is like a tree planted by streams of water, which yields fruit in season.
> Proverbs 31:30 An individual who fears the Lord is to be praised!
> Isaiah 50:4 He awakes me morning by morning with the ear of a disciple, listening like one being taught.

We are called of God to produce individuals who love God's Word and can study it deeply (and teach it effectively) to bring about life transformation.

> Therefore we should begin by choosing/ designing curriculum that can produce an individual who l_____God's Word and can s_____ it deeply(and t_____ it effectively) to bring about life transformation.

The Unmet Need

Why is excellent targeted Bible study curriculum so difficult to find?

The Problem
- A high percentage of published workbooks are written for an "on-the-spot, no h_____" target group because that's what the m_____ will bear.

Excellent Solutions
- Best "targeted" workbooks on the market: for women - Precepts/Kay and LifeWay/Beth

The "Unresolved Mysteries" of the BS Curriculum Search
- What if your target group wants only 2-3 hours of h_____?
- What if your BS format doesn't allow for a one-hour l_____?
- What if you want to bring a friend who has n_____studied the Bible before but you want to study more in-depth?
- How do you find curriculum targeted for both maximum p_____ enjoyment for the Bible student *and* excellent g_____dynamics?

Maximum Enjoyment   **+**   **Excellent**   **=**
for Bible Student   **Group Dynamics**

Satisfied Customer!

One More "Unsolved Mystery": How do you meet the temperament differences of Bible students?

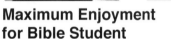

COED AUDIENCE

50% thinkers 50% feelers

FEMALE AUDIENCE

40% thinkers 60% feelers

THINKERS   **FEELERS**   **How will you meet**

What are the necessary ingredients to produce Bible study curricula that results in:

- Maximum personal enjoyment for Bible students
- Excellent group dynamics
- Meeting the needs of both thinkers and feelers
- Meeting the needs of the new Bible student and in-depth learner
- Offering varying homework lengths/depths
- Producing an individual who loves God's Word and can study it deeply (and teach it effectively) to bring about life transformation

The necessary ingredients?

1. Interactive warm-up questions
2. In-depth accurate observation questions
3. Insightful yet accurate interpretation questions based on excellent observation
4. Personal reflective questions that help the text become alive and relevant
5. Excellent correlation questions to correlate the text with other parts of Scripture and relevant life issues
6. Practical measurable application questions that lead to life transformation
7. Multi-level homework in each lesson to allow the new Bible student and the in-depth digger to learn together. For instance:

Just A Moment Questions (10-15 minutes/day)
Core Questions (Unmarked questions - 30 minutes/day)
Digging Deeper (45 minutes/day)

Knowing the necessary ingredients will allow you to:

1. **Recognize** them in a Bible Study workbook when evaluating/choosing curriculum
2. **Distinguish** between "the forest and the trees" with published curriculum
3. **Add** missing ingredients to a Bible study workbook to enhance its effectiveness
3. **Create** new curricula/curriculum with all the necessary ingredients

Often evaluating published curricula is a daunting task because it is challenging to know what to look for. We can tend to get lost in the forest of questions and not be able to distinguish between the individual questions or "the forest and the trees." Understanding and being able to recognize the types of questions will aid in selecting and/or evaluation existing Bible study materials.

TO STUDY SCRIPTURE, WHAT APPROACH SHOULD I TAKE?

There are many ways to study scripture, each with its own strengths and weaknesses. In this leadership course we will be teaching the Inductive Method of Bible study.

A. Deductive Bible Study
1. Begin with principle, theological viewpoint or premise, usually taken from texts outside the Bible, from other teachers or from personal insights.
2. Based on making statements and proving them or backing them up with Scripture.
3. **Result: God speaks to others who speak to you.**

B. Inductive Bible Study
1. Begin with biblical text being studied.
2. Uses Bible as primary text.
3. Based on asking questions of the" text and letting the text speak for itself.
4. Technical term is "exegesis"—drawing out" the meaning of the text.
5. **Result: God speaks to YOU!**

A. The process of learning
1. True learning comes from involvement.
2. Involvement is directly related to the degree to which we raise questions.
3. Questions are the bridge from observations to accurate interpretation.

B. How we hold on to what we learn
1. We retain 70% of what we see.
2. We retain only 15% of what we hear.
3. Writing down our questions helps us organize our data.
4. It also challenges us to use many different kinds of questions.

The process of Inductive Bible Study gets us involved by challenging us to ask questions and develop observations. It reinforces learning by helping us develop the habit of writing down key results from our study.

WHAT ARE THE BASIC STEPS OF INDUCTIVE BIBLE STUDY?

There are many approaches to personal Bible study. The Inductive Bible Study Method we will be using is an orderly, structured approach to understanding and applying scripture. It has four steps:

1. **OBSERVATION** – draw out what the text says

2. **INTERPRETATION** – determine what it means

Exegesis - to draw out the meaning of the text

3. **CORRELATION** – define how the text is connected with the rest of scripture, culture, or my life

4. **APPLICATION** – specify what the text means to me and how it should affect my life in real and specific ways

In the next few pages we will cover each step in detail.

I. OBSERVATION — WHAT THE TEXT SAYS

The purpose of this phase of the inductive study process is to develop a strong sense of the text, to know what it says and be able to explain it to someone else. This phase is the basis for each succeeding one.

OBSERVATION IS THE ART OF SEEING WHAT IS THERE AND ITS SIGNIFICANT. WHAT SHOULD YOU OBSERVE?

I have six faithful serving men who taught me all I know. Their names are what and where and when and how and why and who. **Rudyard Kipling .**

1. **LOOK FOR 5 W's and 1 H**

   - **WHO** wrote it? received it? spoke it? are the main characters and their characteristics?

   - **WHAT** is the main topic? main problem being addressed? are the main events? the event details? the major ideas? are the characters doing? discipline, correction or commendation is being provided?

   - **WHERE** was it written? said? take place? can it be found on a map?

13

- **WHEN** was it written? said? take place? will it happen?

  Mark all references to time with a time symbol:

Now	When
Then	Until
After	Immediately

- **HOW** will it happen? it is done? do the main characters interact? did the passage end? is the outcome shaped?

- **WHY** was it written? was the action taken? (Caution: Only ask why if the text tells you why - otherwise you will be speculating and not truly observing the meaning of the text.)

2. **LOOK FOR KEY WORDS, especially ones that repeat, such as . . .**

God	Riches	Jesus Christ	Heaven
Holy Spirit	Grace	Church	Devil

   1. Key words are words that are either repeated or seem important to the understanding of the text.
   2. Use symbols and/or various colors to mark them.
   3. Make a list for each key word in the margins and draw conclusions.

3. **LOOK FOR CONTRASTS**

   Contrasts are two ideas or concepts that stand in opposition to each other. Consider the contrast between the following two verses:
   - θ Ephesians 2:1 you were dead in your transgressions
   - θ Ephesians 2:4 but God…made us alive with Christ

   Words to look for:

But	However
Yet	Although

   Mark all contrasts with: ≠

4. **LOOK FOR COMPARISONS**

   Comparisons are where the text points out similarities or differences between ideas, concepts, conditions, etc.

   Words to look for:

Like	Also	Likewise
As	So	The same as
Just as	And	

   Mark all comparisons with: ≈

5. & 6. LOOK FOR CONCLUSIONS AND/OR CAUSE AND EFFECT

Conclusions are summary statements; a central point
Cause and effect highlights what caused a situation and what
resulted from it:

Words to look for:

Wherefore	Therefore	Finally
For this reason	Then	So then
So that	Consequently	If, If then

Mark all conclusions or cause and effect with:

7. LOOK FOR GENERAL TO PARTICULAR (or vice versa)

General to particular implies movement in thought from the general or big
picture to the more specific and detailed. No specific "words to look for."
Example of general to particular: Galatians 5:19 "The acts of the sinful
nature are obvious–sexual immorality, etc.
Example of particular to general: Hebrews 11 gives examples of people of
faith and then concludes by saying, "Men of whom the world i not worthy."

8. LOOK FOR PROGRESSION

Progression means that a theme is amplified by additional thoughts,
insights, descriptions or clarifications. Each step of the progression builds
on the one before. The progression often moves to a conclusion. No
specific "words to look for." Example: 2 Peter 1:5 "Add to your faith,
goodness, to goodness knowledge,. . . "

9. LOOK FOR LISTS

SIMPLE LIST - A simple list is found in the passage itself and can be
numbered in the text. Example: Romans 8:35-36 lists that which cannot
separate us from the love of Christ. 1 Timothy 3:2-7 lists the qualifications
of an elder.

TOPICAL LIST A topical list is a comprehensive list of all the words or
phrases that relate to one particular theme or topic in a passage.
Example: Luke 15—lists lost items /John 10—lists descriptions of the
Good Shepherd.

10. WRITE A TITLE FOR EACH PARAGRAPH, CHAPTER AND BOOK

1. Review key word lists, contrasts, comparisons, and conclusions

2. Decide on a summary statement of your own choosing

3. Use a phrase and be concise (2-4 words)

4. Record titles on Scripture Worksheets

NOW IT'S YOUR TURN: Apply the above principles of observation to the following verses. Remember that all ten principles may not apply to every passage.

Observation Practice

Philippians 4:6-7

The text:

"6 Do not be anxious about anything, but in everything, by prayer and petition, with thanksgiving, present your requests to God. 7 And the peace of God, which transcends all understanding, will guard your hearts and your minds in Christ Jesus."

Your Observations: What Do You See?

1. 5 W's and H

2. Key or repeated words

3. Contrasts

4. Comparisons

5. Conclusions

6. Cause and Effect

7. General to Particular or Vice Versa

8. Progression

9. Lists

10. Title for paragraph

II. INTERPRETATION — WHAT THE TEXT MEANS

In this second phase of Inductive Bible Study try to answer the question "What does the text mean?" Interpretation is understanding what the **author** meant without adding your own ideas or insights so as to avoid the sad but true cliché "everyone has their own interpretation of the Bible." In actuality, there is only one true interpretation of a text—the interpretation the author intended for his reading audience.

INTERPRETATION IS THE ART OF UNDERSTANDING THE AUTHOR'S INTENDED MEANING OF THE TEXT. HELPFUL HINTS FOR ACCURATE INTERPRETATION INCLUDE:

1. **ASK FOR THE HELP OF THE HOLY SPIRIT.**

2. **CONSIDER THE SETTING**
   a. Context of the passage
   b. Literary form of the passage
   c. Historical Setting
   d. Cultural Context

3. **CONSIDER THE CONTEXT RULE: Context rules in interpretation.**
   Most, if not all, false interpretations of scripture come because a passage is taken out of context.
   Consider the passage in light of what comes *before and after* the passage you are studying.
   Think or imagine yourself back in the culture, society and time period in which the passage was written.

4. **DETERMINE THE AUTHOR'S INTENDED MEANING FOR HIS OWN HEARERS BEFORE CONSIDERING THE MEANING FOR US TODAY.**

5. **INTERPRET WORDS IN THE USUAL LITERAL SENSE** unless you have reason to believe they are allegorical or figurative. Interpret figures of speech in the same way we use them in normal speech.

6. **STUDY WORD MEANINGS**
For key words, repeated words or any words you cannot define, clearly locate the meaning of the word in a regular dictionary or Bible dictionary.
   a. Find same word in same book.
   b. Find same word by same author.
   c. Find same word in same testament. Find same word in other testament (Septuagint – Greek for the OT)

7. **STUDY GRAMMAR.** ie. verb tenses, singular and plural pronouns, etc.

8. CROSS REFERENCE KEY WORDS OR PHASES. Look up other
scriptures that support, clarify or further explain the Bible passage.
Scripture is the best interpreter of scripture. Draw relationships between
texts. See how one passage helps explain another.
Remember context. It is critical. A verse taken out of context and
"engineered" to support an argument is not God's truth.
Use a **concordance** to look up several references. A concordance might
be found at the back of your Bible; it is a listing of words with reference to
the places they are used in the Bible.

**9. INTERPRET HISTORICAL PASSAGES IN THE LIGHT OF TEACHING
PASSAGES.**
What **did** happen may or may not be what **should** have happened. What
happened for **one** may or may not be for **all**.

**10. INTERPRET THE OLD TESTAMENT IN LIGHT OF THE NEW, AND THE NEW
IN LIGHT OF THE OLD, KEEPING IN MIND GOD'S PROGRESSIVE
REVELATION.**

**11. INTERPRET THE UNCLEAR PASSAGES IN THE LIGHT OF THE CLEAR
PASSAGES.**

**12. CHURCH HISTORY IS IMPORTANT, BUT IT DOES NOT HAVE THE FINAL
WORD. THE WORD OF GOD IS OUR FINAL AUTHORITY FOR FAITH AND
PRACTICE.**

13. CONSIDER FUNDAMENTAL QUESTIONS ASKED OF EVERY PASSAGE:
  • Why did God write this passage and put it in His book?
  • What are the **permanent principles** or **timeless truths** in this passage?
  • What does this passage say about **God**, **Jesus**, the **Holy Spirit**?
  • What does this passage say about **mankind**?
  • What does this passage say about **sin** and **evil**?
  • What does this passage say about **right** or **wrong attitudes**?
  • What does this passage say about **good** or **bad examples?**
  • What does this passage say about **truth** or **error?**

**14. LOOK FOR THE CENTRAL TRUTH, THE MAIN THEME OR THE MAIN POINT
OF THE PASSAGE,** while understanding that the passage will have secondary or
complementary points to the main point of the passage. Look for the
complementary points of the passage as well.

**15. MAKE A LIST OF QUESTIONS WITHOUT TRYING TO ANSWER
THEM AT THIS TIME.** Write down anything that comes to mind that may
eventually need an answer (see next page).

16. ONLY AS A LAST RESORT, CHECK COMMENTARIES (see pages 25-26 for
help in wisely choosing and using commentaries).

Eight types of interpretive questions are given below. Use several questions of each type whenever possible

TYPE	**DESCRIPTION**
Meaning	What does this word or phrase mean?
Significance	What is the significance of this?
Relationship	How are these related to each other?
Identification	Who is this or did this?
Temporal	When was, is, or will this be done?
Local	Where did this happen?
Implication	What does this imply? (also touches on applications)
Rational	Why is this here?

Example questions for Philippians 3:7: "But whatever was to my profit I now consider loss for the sake of Christ."

OBSERVATIONS	INTERPRETIVE QUESTIONS
"but" is a word of contrast	What is contrasted previously to verse 3?
with verses 3-6, "what things" points out specific areas of concern	What specific things is Paul concerned with?
"gain" signifies a previous perspective on things	What does the word gain mean? When were these considered a gain? In what way were they a gain? How can *gain* for Paul be *loss* for Christ?
"have counted" is past tense	What does the word count mean? When did Paul count these as loss? What is involved in counting something as a loss?

Interpretation Practice

NOW IT'S YOUR TURN:

From your previous observations on Philippians 4:6-7 (place in left-hand column), ask interpretive questions as demonstrated on page 20 (principle 15).

Philippians 4:6-7

The text:

"6 Do not be anxious about anything, but in everything, by prayer and petition, with thanksgiving, present your requests to God. 7 And the peace of God, which transcends all understanding, will guard your hearts and your minds in Christ Jesus. "

OBSERVATIONS	INTERPRETIVE QUESTIONS

Interpretation Practice

NOW IT'S YOUR TURN: Apply the sixteen principles of interpretation to the following verses. Remember that all sixteen may not apply to every passage.

16 PRINCIPLES OF INTERPRETATION	
1. Ask for help from Holy Spirit	9. Interpret historical passages in light of teaching passages.
2. Consider the setting.	10. Interpret Old Testament in the light of the new.
3. Consider the context rule.	11. Interpret the unclear passages in light of the clear.
4. Determine the author's intended meaning.	12. Church history is important but it does not have the final word.
5. Interpret words in the usual literal sense.	13. Consider fundamental questions asked of every passage.
6. Study word meanings.	14. Look for the central truth, theme or main point of the passage as well as the complementary points.
7. Study grammar	15. Make a list of questions without trying to answer them.
8. Cross reference key words or phrases.	16. Only as a last resort, check commentaries.

Philippians 4:6-7

The text:

"6 Do not be anxious about anything, but in everything, by prayer and petition, with thanksgiving, present your requests to God. 7 And the peace of God, which transcends all understanding, will guard your hearts and your minds in Christ Jesus. "

Interpretative Insights:

1.

2.

3.

4.

5.

6.

7.

8.

9.

III. CORRELATION — HOW THE TEXT CORRELATES WITH OTHER SCRIPTURES, CULTURE AND WITH MY LIFE PERSONALLY

No section of scripture exists in a vacuum. Rather, it connects to other sections of God's Word, the culture in which it was written, the culture of today, and our lives.

A. Scripture - list how this truth correlates with other scriptures
    1. Old Testament scriptures
    2. New Testament scriptures
    3. Biblical characters as examples (positive and negative)

B. Cultural – how does it correlate with various areas of culture?
    1. Economic
    2. Physical
    3. Political
    4. Recreational
    5. Social
    6. Sexual
    7. Ideological
    8. Psychological

C. Reflective – how does this truth relate to our relationships and past or present experiences?
    1. Spouse
    2. Children
    3. Friends
    4. Neighbors
    5. City
    6. Nation
    7. Workers
    8. World

NOW IT'S YOUR TURN: **Correlate** Philippians 4:6-7 with other parts of Scripture.

"6 Do not be anxious about anything, but in everything, by prayer and petition, with thanksgiving, present your requests to God. 7 And the peace of God, which transcends all understanding, will guard your hearts and your minds in Christ Jesus."

1.

2.

3.

4.

5.

The following two pages contain categories of contextualization for today's issues to

TODAY'S ISSUES FOR CONTEXTUALIZATION OF GOD'S WORD

Personal Interest
➤ **Mental Health**
- ✓ Depression
- ✓ Stress
- ✓ Making Choices
- ✓ Alcoholism
- ✓ Drug Addiction
- ✓ Emotional Problems
- ✓ Crisis issues

➤ **Physical Fitness**
- ✓ Diet and Nutrition
- ✓ Weight Control
- ✓ Exercise

➤ **Spiritual Growth and Renewal**
- ✓ Bible Study
- ✓ Prayer
- ✓ Time issues w/ busy schedules

Personal Relationships
➤ **Friendships**
- ✓ Being a friend
- ✓ Maintaining friendships
- ✓ Loneliness
- ✓ Estrangement in friendships
- ✓ Widowhood and friendships
- ✓ Singleness and Single-parenting and friendships

➤ **Children**
- ✓ Childbirth and preschool age
- ✓ Discipline
- ✓ Stepchildren
- ✓ Blended families
- ✓ Communication
- ✓ Teen morality and pregnancy
- ✓ Grandparents
- ✓ Working Mothers
- ✓ Job sharing to parent effectively

Personal Pain
- ✓ Suicide
- ✓ Pornography
- ✓ Divorce Recovery
- ✓ Widowhood
- ✓ Eating Disorders
- ✓ Domestic Violence
- ✓ Sexual Abuse
- ✓ Lesbianism
- ✓ Abortion Recovery
- ✓ Discontent in Singleness

➤ **Marriage**
- ✓ Marriage preservation
- ✓ Stages of a marriage
- ✓ Late Marriages/ older when having children
- ✓ Marital priority with children
- ✓ Parenting as a team
- ✓ Both partners working

➤ **Extended Family**
- ✓ In- laws
- ✓ Responsibility for parents
- ✓ Caring for the elderly
- ✓ Holiday related issues
- ✓ Grandmother Role

Personal Relationships Cont.
➢ **Divorce**
- ✓ Avoiding divorce
- ✓ Counseling
- ✓ Financial and Legal aspects
- ✓ Divorce Recovery
- ✓ Single parenting
- ✓ Remarriage

➢ **Workplace Relationships**
- ✓ Teamwork in the Workplace
- ✓ Co-ed Working Environments
- ✓ Competition in Relationships
- ✓ Evangelism in the Workplace
- ✓ Friendships VS Working Relationships
- ✓ Balance w/ home/ family/ church

Personal Goals
➢ **Self-improvement**
- ✓ Personality and temperament
- ✓ Self-image
- ✓ Development and use of spiritual gifts
- ✓ Childhood Related Issues
- ✓ Art of Communication
- ✓ Overcoming Boredom
- ✓ Color, clothes, fashion
- ✓ Physical Fitness
- ✓ Personal Mission Statement
- ✓ Goal Setting – 1, 5, 10 year goals

➢ **Suffering from Relationships**
- ✓ Sickness and pain/ care for the care-giver
- ✓ Death and dying
- ✓ Tragedies to loved ones
- ✓ Recovery and Rehabilitation
- ✓ Rape, child-molesting, incest

➢ **Leadership and Job Advancement**
- ✓ Education and training
- ✓ Social Clubs
- ✓ Political Involvement
- ✓ Church Leadership

➢ **Organization**
- ✓ Household
- ✓ Personal
- ✓ Home Decorating
- ✓ Time Management

➢ **Stewardship**
- ✓ God the owner, we the stewards
- ✓ Overall Money Management
- ✓ Giving – How and to What

Correlation Practice

NOW IT'S YOUR TURN: Correlate Philippians 4:6-7 with three issues.

"6 Do not be anxious about anything, but in everything, by prayer and petition, with thanksgiving, present your requests to God. 7 And the peace of God, which transcends all understanding, will guard your hearts and your minds in Christ Jesus.

1.

2.

IV. APPLICATION —— WHAT THE TEXT MEANS TO ME

Application is responding to God's Word—in a personal, active dependent manner, trusting the Holy Spirit to bring about change in our lives.

> "The object of Bible study is changed lives. The Christian world is suffering from a deficiency of Vitamin A - Application. "
> Howard Hendricks

The goal of Bible study, therefore, is the transformation of our lives into ones that please the Father and empowers us to serve others, changing not just *our* lives but the lives of those with whom we interact. In fact, one could define application as "the process of regulating everything we are, everything we think, and everything we do by the Word of God."

Here are some helpful insights about application from the pen of those who love God's Word. The first set (#1-5) come from Susan Rochin, a women's retreat speaker and Bible teacher from California.

#1... General Applications to Ask and Answer

What applications do you see…
- for the church today?
- for Christians in America?
- for men and women in your town or city, both Christ-followers and seekers?
- for those who think God is irrelevant to their lives?

#2... Now to the Nitty Gritty...

What does this passage say to **you** right now in **your** life? Ask **"So what?"** What is this supposed to mean to **me** right now? Think through your relationships, your immediate life circumstances, your emotions and attitudes, and the choices you need to make. Here is a list to get you started:
- **Relationships** (family, friends, neighbors, co-workers, fellow believers)
- **Conflicts** (marriage, children, extended family, work, neighborhood)
- **Personal Burdens** (sickness, death, loss of any kind, family pressures)
- **Difficult Situations** (stress, debt, hindrances, setbacks)
- **Character Weaknesses** (anger, fear, bitterness, lust, selfishness, integrity, image)
- **Lack of Resources** (time, energy, money, materials, information, talents, abilities)
- **Responsibilities** (work and family demands, home projects, church programs, volunteer efforts)
- **Opportunities** (learning, working, serving, moving, traveling)

#3... Apply the Main Point

Write out the **main point** of the passage. It is important to find and apply the **main point** of a passage; otherwise you might find yourself picking and choosing applications that are easy for you and unchallenging. Ask yourself the following:

- **As God is looking at my life today, how well does He think I'm applying this truth?**
- **What would this truth look like if applied to my life?**
- **How would my life be affected if I operated on the basis of this truth? What would change? What would remain the same?**
- What is already part of my thinking?
- What is new to me?
- What requires a change of thought? How can I make the change?
- What is already part of my action?
- What can be applied immediately to my behavior?
- What am I doing that is wrong?
- What action must I take immediately?
- What will I need to do at some future date?

#4... More Questions to Help with Application

- Is there a COMMAND to obey?
- Is there a PROMISE to claim?
- Is there a SIN to confess?
- Is there a WARNING to heed?
- Is there an EXAMPLE to follow?
- Is there an ERROR to avoid or correct?
- Is there an ACTION to take or avoid?
- Is there a HABIT to form or break?
- Is there a TRUTH to be believed?
- Is there an UNTRUTH to be discarded?
- Is there an ATTITUDE to change?
- Is there an ENCOURAGEMENT to speak?
- Is there a PRAYER to pray?
- Is there something to PRAISE?

#5... Pray your Application

Ask the Holy Spirit to help you apply the truth you've learned. Use this passage and some of your cross-references for your daily quiet time.
Consider asking your class to pray for you in regard to your application. Your small group leader will help you write out your request.

#6... Some Dangers of Omitting Application

- You will accumulate facts without grasping their meaning for your life (Ecclesiastes 1:16-18).
- You will substitute emotional experiences for decisions of the will to believe and obey God (2 Corinthians 7:8-11).
- You will not become spiritually mature (Hebrews 5:13-14).
- You will become critical and proud (1 Corinthians 8:1).
- You will deceive yourself and miss the blessing (James 1:22-25).
- You will fall when the hard times come (Luke 6:46-49).

Application Practice

NOW IT'S YOUR TURN: Apply Philippians 4:6-7 using these 6 principles:

Principles of Application
1. General applications to ask: What applications do you see for the church? for Christians in America? your town? both Christ-followers and seekers? for those who think God is irrelevant?
2. Now to the nitty gritty: What does this passage say to you right now? relationships? conflicts? personal burdens? difficult situations? character weaknesses? lack of resources? responsibilities? opportunities?
3. Apply the main point: Is it a part of my thinking? do I need to change an attitude? a behavior?
4. More questions to ask: command to obey? promise to claim? sin to confess? warning to heed? example to follow? error to avoid? action to take? habit to form or break? truth to believe? prayer to pray?
5. Pray your application.
6. Dangers of omitting application.

"6 Do not be anxious about anything, but in everything, by prayer and petition, with thanksgiving, present your requests to God. 7 And the peace of God, which transcends all understanding, will guard your hearts and your minds in Christ Jesus."

1.

2.

3.

4.

5.

6.

SCRIPTURE WORKSHEET
James 1:1-8

₁James, a servant of God and of the Lord Jesus Christ, to the twelve tribes scattered among the nations: Greetings.

Trials and Temptations

₂Consider it pure joy, my brothers, whenever you face trials of many kinds,

₃because you know that the testing of your faith develops perseverance.

₄Perseverance must finish its work so that you may be mature and complete, not lacking anything.

₅If any of you lacks wisdom, he should ask God, who gives generously to all without finding fault, and it will be given to him.

₆But when he asks, he must believe and not doubt, because he who doubts is like a wave of the sea, blown and tossed by the wind.

₇That man should not think he will receive anything from the Lord;

₈he is a double-minded man, unstable in all he does.

1. If your curriculum writing team is writing a workbook based on a teaching passage, complete the above *Scripture Worksheet* by marking the following key words: God (as well as synonyms for God), Jesus Christ (as well as synonyms for Jesus Christ), law, perseveres/perseverance, suffering/testing/endurance/trial.   In the margins, list everything you learn about these words OR You may want to create your own *Scripture Worksheet* taken from the book you will be studying.

2. What other words/and or phrases stand out to you in James 1? Mark these and list everything you learn about them in the margins.

3. Using the *Scripture Worksheet*, mark the following observations:

YOUR OBSERVATIONS? WHAT DO YOU SEE?
1. 5 W's and H
2. Time words
3. Contrasts
4. Comparisons
5. Conclusions
6. Cause and Effect
7. General to Particular (vice versa)
8. Progression
9. LIst
10. Title for paragraphs, for chapter

SCRIPTURE WORKSHEET
Luke 5:12-16

12While Jesus was in one of the towns, a man came along who was covered with leprosy.[a] When he saw Jesus, he fell with his face to the ground and begged him, "Lord, if you are willing, you can make me clean."

13Jesus reached out his hand and touched the man. "I am willing," he said. "Be clean!" And immediately the leprosy left him.

14Then Jesus ordered him, "Don't tell anyone, but go, show yourself to the priest and offer the sacrifices that Moses commanded for your cleansing, as a testimony to them."

15Yet the news about him spread all the more, so that crowds of people came to hear him and to be healed of their sicknesses. **16**But Jesus often withdrew to lonely places and prayed.

1. If your curriculum writing team is writing a workbook based on a narrative passage, complete the above Scripture Worksheet by marking the following key words: Jesus Christ, man with leprosy, willing, news/testimony, etc. In the margins, list everything you learn about these words. OR You may want to create your own *Scripture Worksheet* taken from the book you will be studying.

2. What other words/and or phrases stand out to you in James 1? Mark these and list everything you learn about them in the margins.

3. Using the Scripture Worksheet, mark the following observations:.

YOUR OBSERVATIONS? WHAT DO YOU SEE?
1. 5 W's and H
2. Time words
3. Contrasts
4. Comparisons
5. Conclusions
6. Cause and Effect
7. General to Particular (vice versa
8. Progression
9. LIsts
10.Title for paragraphs, for chapter

THE SCIENCE AND ART OF ASKING QUESTIONS OF ASKING QUESTIONS

"Study the Bible in such a way when we are together, that people can be encouraged to study the Bible on their own as well."

Source unknown

The Science of Asking Questions

Remember that the role of the small group leader is to be (1) a stimulator of personal fellowship; and (2) a guide in discovering the truth of God, rather than simply declaring the truth of God. Flow questions can assist you in carrying out each of these roles. There are four main types of questions that make up the flow:

- Warm up: "Let's get better acquainted"
- Observation: "What does the text say?"
- Interpretative: "What does the text mean?
- Correlation: "How does the text correlate with other Scripture, my life, culture?"
- Application: "How do I respond?"

Flow questions are a series of questions composed and arranged in such a way as to lead a person from discovering what a passage says to understanding and applying one or two portions of it to one's daily life in a specific way. The questions are based on one's personal study of the text.

I. Warm-up Questions - A bridge from our world to the Biblical world that accomplishes the goal of "Let's get better acquainted."

A. Developing your warm-up questions
1. Identify the main ideas of a text
2. Choose area(s) on which you will focus the application
3. Choose a warm-up question that will prepare the group for the discussion of that area.
4. Be sure the question has a clear tie to a subject or idea in the text.

Example for Philippians 2:5-12: When have you slipped into a role that is not natural to you in order to serve or do something good for someone else?

A. Select warm-up questions that will help the group become better acquainted with one another. For example:
    1. What heroes did you admire as a child? (If studying life of David)
    2. Or, what are the qualities that you appreciate in a friend? (John 15)

B. Warm-up questions can go deeper as the group gets better acquainted; but in the initial stages of group development, warm-up questions should:
    1. Be fairly easy to answer.
    2. Help people to become comfortable talking with one another.
    3. Well-written warm-up questions should allow the Bible study participant to tell a short story.

II. Observation Questions "What does the text say?"

A. Observation questions aim to increase one's knowledge of the text since interpretation, correlation, and application are based on accurate and full observation of what the text says.

B. Observation questions should:

1. Deal with the key ideas and associated detail germane to the key idea
2. Take your group into the teaching or events of the passage.
3. Help the group reconstruct the passage in the words of the text and then in their own words.

C. Do not overlook the observation step:
1. Even though the answers may appear obvious to you.
2. Because careful observation provides the foundation for accurate interpretation.
3. Observation enables appropriate correlation and application.

D. Observation questions should:
    1. Have several answers, each easily discernible from thoughtful reading of the text.
    2. Be chosen so that everyone can participate freely from the outset of the biblical discussion.
    3. **Often use a plural noun** to reinforce several right answers (i.e. insights, blessings, characteristics, promises, commands, etc.)
    4. Avoid one-word answers.

    Example: 1 Corinthians 13

Example: Mark 2:1-12

> | Observation
> | Questions take
> | answers
> | straight from
> | the text.

θ Not – How many friends helped the paralyzed man through the roof?

θ But – "What needs did Jesus meet in this passage of individuals and of groups of people?"

A. Determine the number of observation questions by the desired length and depth of the homework (i.e. digging deeper homework may have several more than core question homework).

B. As far as possible:
1. Use the phrasing of the text in the wording of your questions.
2. Encourage your group to cite the verse first, then answer in the wording of the text before attempting to paraphrase.
3. These are especially important if different translations are being used.

III. Interpretation Questions "What does the text mean?" (also called Understanding Questions)

A. Interpretation Questions focus on the meaning of the text by enabling you to **draw out implications** or **conclusions** about the text.

B. Interpretation Questions may also **define a word** or its context.

C. Avoid questions that are speculative or unnecessarily controversial.

> **How to tell the difference between an Observation Question & an Interpretation Question**
>
> Observation Questions take answers straight from the text.
> You don't have to interpret the text. Interpretation Questions you do have to

1. They can divert and subvert rather than foster spiritual growth and fellowship.
2. For example, "What did Paul feel like when he apologized to the Corinthians?" (2 Corinthians 1:12-24). If Paul brings this up, then you can. If not, leave it alone.

D. As with the other discussion questions:
1. Ask questions that promote discussion.
2. Avoid one-word answers that can close a group down.
3. Use interpretation questions that require more than a one-word or "yes-or-no" answer.
4. Reword such questions to change them away from one-word style.

Example:
Not – "Was God pleased with Jonah's response?"
But – "What does God's handling of Jonah reveal about the character of God?"

IV. Correlation Questions ("How do these ideas compare to other Scriptures, experiences from my life, or today's culture?")

Correlation Questions typically follow an observation or interpretation question and help to clarify or bring deeper or broader insight to the text being studied. There are three types of Correlation Questions:

A. **Scriptural Correlation Questions** – These connect the present passage with other passages in Scripture that help shed light on the present passage.

   1. Like observation and interpretation questions, they should have several right answers and promote discussion, even if answers are taken from several different portions of Scripture.

   2. They serve as "thinking questions and minister to the "upper levels" of the mind, enabling the Bible student to acquire greater knowledge about the original passage being addressed.

      Example: Philippians 2:5-11 How do the following passages shed light on the quality of humility introduced in this passage?

      1 Peter 5 5:8   James 4:9-10   Titus 3:2

   3. Scriptural correlation questions typically follow an observation or interpretation question and help to clarify or bring deeper or broader insight to the text being studied.

      For example: Philippians 4:6-7 What elements of Paul's command are suggested as an antidote to anxiety? (Observation Question).

      What insights do the following scriptures give us into why Paul might feel that thanksgiving should be at the front end of any request we make to God? (Scriptural Correlation Question)
      1 Corinthians 15:57 2 Corinthians 2:14 Ephesians 5:20

   4. Scriptural Correlation Questions are one of the main tools that can be used to create longer more in-depth homework for Bible participants (Digging Deeper).

B. **Cultural Correlation Questions** – These connect the present passage with perspectives found in our culture or in our world around us. They help us consider how our own thinking has changed or developed since we have met the Lord.

Example: Genesis 4:1-14 To what extent do today's counselors put blame on the environment for bad behavior?

C. **Reflective (Correlation) Questions** - These cause us to take the knowledge of the text and interpret it by reflecting it back into one's life. They help **"life touch life"** and **enable the feeler to "feel involved."**

They connect the biblical world to our world by bringing our lives in review. They **take the discussion to the heart level,** out of the realm of the head and thinking level **through the sharing of personal experience.**

Without them, the **only time "life touches life"** would be at the **beginning of the study** (warm-up question) and at the **end** (application question).

Example: Philippians 4:3-10 "Which of these ideas played a major part in your life when you experienced conflict with another believer?"

Example: Philippians 4:3-10 "How have you personally experienced one of these principles at work on a church committee? In your home? At work?"

They can do one or all of the following (examples from Genesis 1:1-2:3 and Genesis 2:4-5).

a) Enable you to reflect about a **previous life experience** (i.e. *Describe an experience you've had in nature that reminds you of how you would have visualized the earth appearing at its outset?*

b) Enable you to s**hare or reflect your feelings about the knowledge** you have gained from the passage (i.e. *As you look around at God's creation, how does it give you a greater appreciation for the Creator?*)

c) Enable you to **reflect about your present life in light of what you are learning** (i.e. *Note the social dimension of being created in the image of God (v. 18). What implications does this have for your relationships with other people?*)

V. **Application Questions** are designed to help a person apply one's understanding of a passage to daily life in a specific way. Application questi would lead to the exercise of obedience and faith in response to God's truth

Good Application Questions should lead to the setting of a measurable goal in applying the Word of God. Because it is stated as a question, it still leaves room for the Spirit's leading in individual lives (Example of application which does not leave room for the Spirit's leading; To avoid bei conformed to this world (Romans 12:1-2), let's all not use our TV's this wee be on the net.

A. Application Questions yield answers that are:
   1. Measurable,
   2. Achievable within a specific period of time, such as one week or one month.

B. Application Questions remind us that:
   1. Life change comes from obeying the Word of God
   2. We must act, not just know it intellectually.
   3. Two-parted application questions are often needed, one question to narrow to one aspect of the Bible participant's life and the second to narrow to one step or one action to take this week or month.

   Example: Philippians 4:6-7
   θ "What worry will you commit to God in prayer each day this week?"
   θ "What positive step can you take to be faithful in prayer this week for the things that worry you?"

C. Also consider the following in writing and using good Application Questions:
   1. See what application the Biblical writer makes. Translate those into present day terminology.

   2. Sometimes applications can be implemented within the small group itself. "What expression of encouragement would you like to share with another member of the group right now?"

   3. Encourage individuals to share in the group how they tried to apply the previous week's lessons to real life situations. Encourage free expression of failure as well as successes.

   4. Link the sharing of applications with conversational prayer. These are the very areas in which we need one another's prayer, or for which others can join us in praise.

LEARNING TO IDENTIFY GOOD QUESTIONS

Examples of Warm up Questions

Please match each of the following questions with a, b, or c.
a. Warm up Questions too deep for new group
b. A Warm up Question that will NOT lead to personal sharing
c. Excellent Warm up question for a new group

1 Samuel 1—Hannah longs for a child
1. Describe a time when you asked God for something you really wanted and He gave it to you. What was it and how did His "yes" answer make you feel?
2. Share a time when you were really depressed. What was the result of your depression?
3. What are symptoms of depression? What do people do when they are depressed?

Examples of Observation Questions

Please match each of the following questions with a, b, or c.
a. Good Observation Question: many answers, will promote discussion
b. Too narrow of an Observation Question: will not promote discussion
c. Not an observation question

Ephesians 1:1-14—Spiritual Blessings from our Heavenly Father
1. What are the spiritual blessings Paul lists in these verses? (List as many as you can). What reasons does Paul give for God having given you these blessings?

      Spiritual Blessings   Reasons

2. Verse 5 reveals that you have been "adopted" by God. According to this verse, why did God "adopt" you?
3. When were the Ephesians chosen to belong to God?
4. With each of these spiritual blessings Paul indicates a time frame in which God gives them (past, present, future). Next to your list of blessings, indicate what you can discover from the text about the timing of the giving of each gift.
5. What words or phrases in this passage reveal Paul's emotions as he is writing?
6. What does it mean to be "blessed in the heavenly realms?" See Eph. 1:20 and 2:6 for additional insight.

Examples of Interpretation Questions

Please match each of the following questions with a, b, or c.
a. Good Interpretation Question: many answers, will promote discussion
b. Too narrow of an Interpretation Question: will not promote discussion
c. Not an Interpretation Question

1 Samuel 1—Hannah longs for a child

1. What do the actions of Elkanah (Hannah's husband) reveal about his character? His capacity to be a good husband?
2. How did Hannah handle the provoking from Pinnenah (Elkanah's other wife)? What steps did she take to cope with her sorrow?
3. Hannah was described as a woman with "bitterness of soul." Is it ever appropriate for a Christian woman to experience such bitterness? Why or why not?

Examples of Correlation Questions

Please match each of the following questions with a, b, or c.
a. Good Scriptural Correlation Question
b. Good Cultural Correlation Question
c. Good Reflective (Correlation) Question

Ephesians 1:1-14—Spiritual Blessings from our Heavenly Father

1. When recently have you given a special gift to one of your children (or to a close friend) and have them receive it as a blessing? How did it make you feel?
2. What similarities are there between our spiritual adoption and an earthly adoption? What differences are there between the two?
3. If you have any personal experience with adoption, please share your insights with the group.
4 What additional insights into our adoption by God (v.5) do the following passages give?

Galatians 3:26-29   Romans 8:15-16
Galatians 4:5-7   Romans 8:23

Examples of Application Questions

Please match each of the following questions with a, b, or c.

a. Good measurable, achievable Application Question
b. Poor Application Question, not measurable or achievable
c . Not an Application Question

1 Samuel 1—Hannah longs for a child

1. Where in your life right now are you waiting on God? What is one lesson you have learned from Hannah's "waiting room experience" that you could apply to your life? What is one step you could take this week to apply it?
2. What is the one thing that has helped you the most as you have waited on God in the past? Share with us the instance and what you learned from it.
3.. What can you learn from Hannah about how to handle those who provoke you?

Now it's your turn: To help you practice how to write each type of question, create the following questions for James 1:1-8 without considering the flow. Write out brief answers to these questions. Answering your own questions will help you discover the adequacy or inadequacy of each question.

Flow Questions Practice One

One Warm-Up Question
1.

Three Observation Questions
1.

2.

3.

Two Interpretation Questions
1.

2.

Three Correlation Questions (One scriptural correlation question, one cultural correlation question plus two reflective correlation questions)
1.

2.

3.

4.

One Application Question
1.

Now it's time to take the next step in creating a set of flow questions. On the next page, ***rearrange your questions into a logical flow***, starting with a warm-up question and ending with an application question. Each interpretation question should logically follow an observation question. Each correlation question should follow either an interpretation question or an observation question. In your set of flow questions, you may or may not include all of the above questions.

To create the flow, you may need to add additional questions not included on this page. As you write, imagine an individual or group gleaning from your questions, as they move logically and/or emotionally from one question to the next.

Text: James 1:1-8

Major Subject: _____

Flow Questions Practice Two

Write one set of flow questions for the text stated above, ***creating the logical flow as you write.*** Aim to include most of following in your set: one Warm-Up Question, two to three Observation Questions, at least two Interpretation Questions, one Scriptural or Cultural Correlation Question, one Reflective Question, one Application Question, arranged in a logical flow.

1.

2.

3.

4.

5.

6.

7.

8.

9.

10.

Now it's your turn: To help you practice how to write each type of question, create the following questions for Luke 5:12-16 without considering the flow. Write out brief answers to these questions. Answering your own questions will help you discover the adequacy or inadequacy of each question.

Flow Questions Practice Three

One Warm-Up Question
1.

Three Observation Questions
1.

2.

3.

Two Interpretation Questions
1.

2.

.

Three Correlation Questions (One scriptural correlation question, one cultural correlation question plus two reflective correlation questions)
1.

2.

3.

4.

One Application Question
1.

Now it's time to take the next step in creating a set of flow questions. On the next page, **rearrange your questions into a logical flow**, starting with a warm-up question and ending with an application question. Each interpretation question should logically follow an observation question. Each correlation question should follow either an interpretation question or an observation question. In your set of flow questions, you **may or may not include all of the above questions.**

To create the flow, you may need to **add** additional questions not included on this page. As you write, imagine an individual or group gleaning from your questions, as they move logically and/or emotionally from one question to the next.

40

Text: Luke 5:12-16

Major Subject: _____

Flow Questions Practice Four

Write one set of flow questions for the text stated above, ***creating the logical flow as you write***. Aim to include most of following in your set: one Warm-Up Question, two to three Observation Questions, at least two Interpretation Questions, one Scriptural or Cultural Correlation Question, one Reflective Question, one Application Question.

1.

2.

3.. .

Template for:

supply name of study

OVERVIEW OF LESSON/DAY (1-3)	check list
1. **EACH LESSON SHOULD HAVE a clearly stated purpose and time requirements** – 5 days, CORE = 6 pages, 1 ½ -2 hours of homework. TOTAL LESSON with 2 pages of digging deeper questions = 8 pages (6 of CORE, 2 of DD), 3 – 4 hours of total homework, 1-1 1/2 hours for DD	
2. **OVERVIEW EVALUATION of EACH DAY:** In any given day, create at least 1-2 observation questions, at least 1 interpretation question, and at least 1 feeling question—3 of the 5 days the feeling question should be a reflective question/2 of the 5 days the feeling question should be an application question. These rules can be broken.	
3. **EACH LESSON and EACH DAY should have a** good balance of thinking and feeling questions. How intellectually involved were you in the lesson? 1 2 3 4 5 Not involved very involved How emotionally involved were you in the lesson? 1 2 3 4 5	
OVERVIEW OF TYPES OF QUESTIONS (4-8)	
4. **WARM-UP QUESTIONS SHOULD BE . . .** Condensed warm-ups/ not multi-layered "ice-breaker," not deep self-evaluative	
5. **RULE FOR SCRIPTURAL CORRELATION QUESTIONS IN THE CORE . . . at LEAST 2, at MOST 3** If only 2, may use more references. If 3, use less references. Be sensitive to how many cross references you use because DD will also use cross references. **THIS RULE CAN BE BROKEN.**	

6. **All 5 days should have at least ONE FEELING QUESTION.**
• **TWO DAYS should have a PRAYER OR APPLICATION QUESTION. TWO PRAYER OR APPLICATION QUESTIONS REQUIRED PER LESSON.** Possibilities for prayer questions might include
    a. Thank God today for . . .
    b. Intercede today for . . .
    c. Praise God today for (some aspect of God's nature studied in your passage.
    d. Confess today about
    e. Ask God today for
• **THREE DAYS should have a REFLECTIVE QUESTION,** *possibly* placed at the end of the day. You may place it somewhere else in the flow of the day. The choice is yours.
• **IN CONCLUSION,** each day **MUST** have at least one feeling question (warm-up, reflective, or prayer/application question.)
• **If possible,** DAY 5 PRAYER OR APPLICATION QUESTION should try to review or cover entire lesson.
This rule is meant to be broken. Do not get legalistic as these are only meant to serve as helpful guidelines for a good lesson.	

7. To what degree were you able to apply the lesson to your own life?
                      1   2   3   4   5
                not applicable very applicable	

8. On one day, you *may* acknowledge **various way(s) to APPLY or respond to the truth.** Write a prayer, draw a picture, create a story, a poem, write a letter etc. Feel free to ask for just ONE of these responses or all of these. The choice is up to you.	

DIGGING DEEPER (9)	check list
9. 2 pages of Digging Deeper. Digging Deeper questions *may* include: Scriptural correlation questions, word studies, use of cross-references, cumulative charts, etc. DD questions focus on one specific aspect of the lesson. They expand the knowledge of that aspect through Scriptural correlation, OCCASIONAL use of concordances, Bible dictionaries or commentaries (no more than one per lesson). A DD question often starts with: Read the following passages and note… or Using a Bible concordance locate passages about … If you have an important concept you would like to address but it can't be addressed in the CORE, use DD to address such issues.	
GENERAL RULES (10-14) BIBLE REFERENCES, CHARTS, DAY TITLES, TRANSITIONS, ETC.	
10. Wherever biblical insights are shared, **ALWAYS give BIBLE REFERENCES**. Bold all references, Please do NOT say, "Scripture teaches . . ." without giving a reference.	
11. **Study NOTES as addenda rather than in text** Please create them as a separate document.	
12. For **CHARTS**, give enough writing space. Some charts may need a filled-in example to help the Bible student understand how to fill in the rest of the chart	
13. DAY TITLES have been preliminarily chosen for you. Day titles should ALWAYS be stated as applying to the reader. See suggested day titles for your lesson. Day titles are not in cement. If you choose to change them, please try to maintain the parallel nature of the 5 days.	
14. Add **TRANSITIONS** (statements or short paragraphs), if necessary, to clarify the flow of the lesson.	

Team Assignments

Writing Team	Lesson Title Written as Application for Bible Student	Author of Unnumbered Page

Sample of This Year's Curriculum

Sample of Application-Oriented Lesson Titles:

Lesson One (Ps. 8, 19, 29, 139)
Marveling at God's Creation

Lesson Two (Ps. 131, 23, 8, 3, 46)
Resting in God's Care

Lesson Three (Ps. 27, 42, 43, 63)
Thirsting After God in Times of Stress

Lesson Four (Ps. 1, 51, 73, 18, 90)
Living Out the Psalms' Wisdom

Lesson Five (Ps. 120-134)
Ascending in Praise through the
Pilgrim Psalms

Lesson Six (Ps.103, 107, 136, 116, 92)
Increasing in Contentment through
Thanksgiving

Lesson Seven (Ps. 55, 137, 18, 62)
Being Real in Victory and Defeat

Lesson Eight (Ps. 45, 22, 2, 110)
Deepening in Love for the Messiah

Lesson Nine (Ps. 40, 71, 78, 92, 96)
Declaring God's Glory

Sample of Application-Oriented Day Titles

Day One: Psalm 8
Humbled by God's Majestic Creation

Day Two: Psalm 19
Experiencing a Heart Change as a Result
of God's Spoken and Silent Revelations

Day Three: Psalm 29
Listening to God's Voice in Creation

Day Four: Psalm 29
Giving Glory to God for His Kingship Over
Creation

Day Five: Psalm 139
Praising the Creator and Searcher of My
Inmost Soul

The Five-Day Meeting Plan for Curriculum Writing

People lead busy lives. The five-day meeting plan has been created to minimize meetings and maximize effective production of curriculum.

DAY 1
CWT Team Introduced
CWT Taught the **BASICS OF CURRICULUM WRITING**
> **THE WHY:** Why write curriculum? The Target on the Wall
> **THE HOW:** Mastering basic tools needed for curriculum writing
> > Biblical Skills:and Flow Question Skills

CWT Receive Biblical Assignments, Five Day Lesson with Day-Titles and
> Writer/Helper Team-Mate Assignments

BETWEEN DAY 1 & DAY 2
Writers/Helpers complete biblical work (individually)
Writer complete commentary work
Writers/Helpers individually dream/pray about 5-Day Lesson in light of Day Titles

DAY 2
CWT **Review Types of Questions**
CWT introduced to Extra Helps for Creating Good Questions
Writer/Helper Pairs meet to **dream/brainstorm/pray about ideas** for 5-Day Lesson in light of provided Day Titles
Writer/Helper Pairs introduced to templates

BETWEEN DAY 2 & DAY 3
Writer write lesson/Helper give feedback
Writer make corrections to her lesson from helper feedback prior to CWT DAY 3

DAY 3
CWT meet in 4's---2 Writer/Helper Pairs meet to present rational for their lessons

BETWEEN DAY 3 & DAY 4
Each Writer/helper pair edit/agree on feedback to give on swapped lesson

DAY 4
CWT Coached on how to give feedback
CWT meet in 4's to give feedback on edited lessons

BETWEEN DAY 4 & DAY 5
Writer of each lesson incorporate edits into final draft of lesson

DAY 5
CWT turn in final lessons by email and hard copy to Editing Team
CWT evaluate personal and team learning curves/
CWT make list of take-aways/what we'll do differently next year
CWT celebrate the completed project passed on to the editing team

The following is an example of an email to be sent to each paired curriculum writing team (one writer/one helper) introducing them to their team assignment. The following documents should be attached.

1. Template for your lesson
2. Template for introductory page (unnumbered)
3. Template for Study Notes
4. Template for Bibliography
5. Instructions for working on your lesson

Welcome to your **FIRST CURRICULUM WRITING TEAM ASSIGNMENT FOR**

name of study)   to be completed by April _____ (rough draft)

Assignments are *manageable* and *with some hard work and leadership from the Holy Spirit, easily obtainable* within the suggested time limits!

The mail goal is to *stay on task*! If you do, you will complete the rough draft of your lesson on time by _____ .
(suggested due date for final draft in late May, early June)

The unnumbered page for your lesson will be written by _____ .
(either by you or a designated writer on specializes in writing unnumbered pages)

Upon completion of your lesson on May/June _____, the editing team will review the lessons. They will next go to _____ for FINAL fine-line grammatical editing. Once FINAL editing is completed, _____ will finalize format.

We are on a publication deadline so that all of us can take a good portion of the summer off! Please meet deadlines **on time** so as NOT to slow down those working on the end product!

REVIEW OF DUE DATES FOR PUBLICATION:

Rough Draft Due	April _____
Final Draft Due	May/June _____
Editing Team Final Edits Due	July 1
Fine-Line Editing Completed	July 15
Finalize Formatting	August 1
Curriculum Xeoxed/Collated	by August 15
Women's Bible Study Registration Begins	3rd weekend in August

Prayerfully and with great expectations of a job well done to glory of God,

Sample Lesson Template

Header should read:

Theme for Year   **Title of this Workbook**
Burstin' with Praise, Blossomin' in Prayer, Bloomin' in Wisdom   Experiencing God in the Psalms

Lesson Two ~ Resting In God's Care

Warm-Up:

Day One: Remaining Still in Abba Daddy's Arms

1A. **Read Psalm 131,** *a psalm of confidence.*

Day Two: Following the Good Shepherd by Still Waters

2A. **Read Psalm 23,** *a psalm of confidence.*

Day Three: Finding Safe Refuge through All of Life's Seasons

3A. **Read Psalm 16,** *a psalm of confidence.*

Day Four: Experiencing God's Shield with Uplifted Head

4A. **Read Psalm 3,** *a psalm of confident expression of trust in God's goodness and power.*

Day Five: Relying On My Ever-Present Help in Times of Trouble

5A. **Read Psalm 46.**

Footer should read:
Copyright@2010 by Grace Baptist Church WOW Hudson, MA   Lesson One: Page One

To aid in overall consistency of the final product and to avoid redundancy, it may be helpful to email templates for each of the lessons to the entire team for the sake of cross-checking day titles and pre-assigned passages..

Sample Introductory or Unnumbered Page Template

Header should read:

Theme for Year   **Title of this Workbook**
Burstin' with Praise, Blossomin' in Prayer, Bloomin' in Wisdom   Experiencing God in the Psalms

Lesson One/Two etc. ~ Title for Unnumbered Page

Footer should read:
Copyright@2010 by Grace Baptist Church WOW Hudson, MA   Lesson One: Introduction

Sample Study Notes Template (to be located at end of each 5-Day lesson)

Header should read:

Theme for Year   **Title of this Workbook**
Burstin' with Praise, Blossomin' in Prayer, Bloomin' in Wisdom   Experiencing God in the Psalms

Lesson One ~ Title of Your Lesson
Study Notes

Study Note #1: Day One, Question 1A etc.

Footer should read:
Copyright@2010 by Grace Baptist Church WOW Hudson, MA   Lesson One: Study Notes

Sample Bibliography Template (located at end of Bible Study workbook)
oHeader should read:

Theme for Year   **Title of this Workbook**
Burstin' with Praise, Blossomin' in Prayer, Bloomin' in Wisdom   Experiencing God in the Psalms

Bibliography

Bibles

The NIV Study Bible. Grand Rapids: Zondervan Publishing House, 2002

Books

Eareckson Tada, Joni. *The Joni Story.* London: Marshall Pickering, 1996.

Greig, Pete. *God on Mute: Engaging the Silence of Unanswered Prayer.* California: Regal Books, 2007.

Clip Art

Unnumbered Page: *Picture of Injured Man*:
http://www.centerimt.com/images/people/FirstStep/T10c---mike-long_large.jpg

Website

http://www.biblegateway.com/resources/commentaries/index.php?
action=getCommentaryText&cid=6&source=1&seq=i.54.11.2

Footer should read: Bibliography
Copyright@2010 by Grace Baptist Church WOW Hudson, MA

*Instructions for **working on emailed document** of your lesson:*

1. Your emailed document has been prepared according to a standard template for Bible Study Curriculum. The font sizes and the types of fonts have all been chosen for you.

2. The margins have been preset at .8 top, bottom, right, left.

3. Please do NOT make changes to the fonts or to the margins. If you do NOT have Lucinda Bright italics on your computer (for lesson and day titles), your computer will automatically default to a different font. Use whatever font to which it defaults. I will make changes when you email me the final document. Do not try to change the font to look like the original hard copy we give to you.

4. If you want to include a chart in your lesson, please type in the directions. DO NOT TRY TO CREATE THE CHART ON YOUR COMPUTER. Do not add text boxes. Feel free to draw the chart for me, letting me know about how much room you want for each column and/row.

5. If you would like to help with formatting YOUR LESSON, please do so ONLY according to formatting instructions on page 66 entitled WOW Curriculum Formatting Instructions).

6. Please do NOT add clip art. Clip art must be well documented. If you have an idea for clip art, please describe it or send a picture as an example.

7. According to correct protocol, only one space is necessary after every period. Since most of us learned to type with a 2nd space after every period, we will create our whole document with a 2 space format even though it is technically no longer correct.

8. Please DO NOT try to format the numbering. Just hit return and type the next number as this document shows. The formatter will format all numbering as part of the final document. Please do NOT do the following. It will NOT be helpful:

    1. Question one. Fjggkb kfmfkobovoofmfkgjmbkk b kfgjgjkkj mfnmfkgkggfmgmmbbmbmbmbmbmbmgvgmfmffmfm

    2. Question two Finddkilsdklsn'cvnn'lkfmnm'smnslkfns vcnvnnvvnvn lklkfns'kfnsdfsldkdfmsdkdf

9. **All curriculum writing team participants should receive a copy of your lesson document—WRITERS *AND* HELPERS. Save the document. Make a 2nd copy of the document and save it. Please feel free to enter your changes into your 2nd copy. Please keep the original to remind you of where you began.**

Lesson Plan Curriculum Writing Team Day 2
Date _____

Time Schedule	Agenda	Page #	Summary of Homework to be completed by May ___
9:15-9:25	One insight you gleaned from your lesson that blessed you, touched your life, or you've been meditating on!		**Writer** 1. WRITE YOUR LESSON in light of agreed upon template. Make changes to the original emailed document from here on. DO NOT CHANGE FORMAT (see added formatting instructions). 2. Email to helper by agreed upon date. 3. Receive feedback (POSITIVE/then CONSTRUCTIVE) from your helper by phone or in person. 4. Agree upon changes, although writer has final word. 5. Make changes to original document. Email adjusted document to partner in timely fashion to bring partner up to speed. Bring 3 copies of document to class.
9:25-9:50	**Review:** Types of questions **Introduce:** Extra helps for creating good questions (PULL OUT 3 PAGES PUT IN FRONT OF MANUAL) **Reintroduce:** Instructions for working on the emailed document of your lesson **Introduce:** Curriculum Formatting Instructions	56 59 61 63 65 66	
9:50-9:55	Any template questions or concerns at this point?		
9:55-11:15	Meet in pairs and complete today's assignment: **Writer's Task:** 1. Review lesson together with helper. 2. Share insights related to BIG PICTURE EVALUATION. 3. Decided on date to email lesson to helper **Helper's Task:** 1. Review lesson together with writer. 2. Respond to writer's insights related to BIG PICTURE EVALUATION. 3. Share your own insights related to same. 4. Agree upon an email date		**Helper** Receive emailed lesson. 1. Complete lesson, answering all questions, checking all passages for accuracy, questions for clarity, lesson for T-F flow and balance etc. according to template. 2. Talk by phone or in person, giving honest POSITIVE and then CONSTRUCTIVE feedback to your writer. 3. Receive emailed adjusted copy of lesson from writer in time to review prior to _____. Bring two draft copies to class and any lingering questions you may still have regarding your lesson.
11:15-11:45	Regather as whole team Any suggestions? Questions? PRAY & GO		

REVIEW OF TYPES OF QUESTIONS

I. Warm-Up Questions - A bridge from our world to the Biblical world that accomplishes the goal of "Let's get better acquainted."

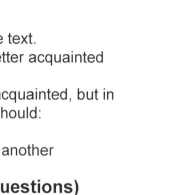

Helpful hints in developing good warm-up questions:
1. Identify the main ideas of a text
2. Choose area(s) on which you will focus the application
3. Choose a warm-up question that will prepare the group for the discussion of that area.
4. Be sure the question has a clear tie to a subject or idea in the text.
5. Select warm-up questions that will help the group become better acquainted with one another.
6. Warm-up questions can go deeper as the group gets better acquainted, but in the initial stages of group development, warm-up questions should:
    a. Be fairly easy to answer
    b. Help people to become comfortable talking with one another

II. Observation Questions (also called Understanding Questions) "What does the text say?"

1. Observation questions aim to increase one's knowledge of the text since interpretation, correlation, and application are based on accurate and full observation of what the text says.
2. Observation questions should:
    a. Have several answers, each easily discernible from thoughtful reading of the text.
    b. Be chosen so that everyone can participate freely from the outset of the biblical discussion.
    c. As much as possible, use the phrasing of the text in the wording of your questions.
    d. Help the group reconstruct the passage in the words of the text and then in their own words.
    e. Avoid most one-answer questions. Some one-answer questions can be helpful, but they should be more the exception than the rule. One answer questions do not promote discussion.

III. Interpretation Questions (also called Understanding Questions) "What does the text mean?"

1. Interpretation Questions focus on the meaning of the text by enabling you to draw out implications or conclusions about the text.
2. Avoid questions that are speculative or unnecessarily controversial as they can divert and subvert rather than foster spiritual growth and fellowship.

3. As with the other discussion questions:
   a. Ask questions that promote discussion
   b. Avoid one-word answers that can close a group down.
   c. Use interpretation questions that require more than a one-word or "yes-or-no" answer.
   d. Reword such questions to change them away from one-word style.

IV. Correlation Questions ("How do these ideas compare to other Scriptures, experiences from my life, or today's culture?")

1. **Scriptural Correlation Questions** - connect the present passage with other passages in Scripture that help shed light on the present passage. *Scriptural Correlation Questions are one of the main tools that can be used to create longer more in-depth homework for Bible participants (Digging Deeper).*

2. **Cultural Correlation Questions** – These connect the present passage with perspectives found in our culture or in our world around us. They help us consider how our own thinking has changed or developed since we have met the Lord.

3. **Reflective (Correlation) Questions** - These connect the Biblical world to our world by bringing our lives in review. They help "life touch life" and enable the feeling individual to feel involved in the discussion through the sharing of personal experience. They take the discussion to the heart level, out of the realm of the head and thinking level. Without them, the only time "life touches life" would be at the beginning of the study (warm-up question) and at the end (application question).

VI. Application Questions yield answers that are:

1. Measurable.
2. Achievable within a specific period of time, such as one week or one month.
3. Application questions remind us that life change comes from obeying the Word of God and that we must act, not just know it intellectually.

60

Good Observation Questions Created with Plural Nouns

1. Accomplishments
2. Accusations
3. Acts
4. Actions
5. Affirmations
6. Answers
7. Applications
8. Arguments
9. Aspects
10. Attitudes
11. Barriers
12. Behaviors
13. Beliefs
14. Benefits
15. Blessings
16. Celebrations
17. Challenges
18. Characteristics
19. Choices
20. Circumstances
21. Commands
22. Comparisons
23. Compassions
24. Concerns
25. Conclusions
26. Confessions
27. Confirmations
28. Consequences
29. Contrasts
30. Costs/Benefits
31. Creations
32. Curses
33. Dangers
34. Descriptions
35. Desires
36. Differences
37. Discoveries
38. Dissatisfactions
39. Disturbances
40. Effects
41. Elements
42. Emotions
43. Encouragements
44. Essentials
45. Events
46. Evaluations
47. Evidences of belief, unbelief
48. Examples
49. Experiences
50. Expressions
51. Facts
52. Failures

53. Fears
54. Feelings
55. Frustrations
56. Gains
57. Generalities
58. Grievances
59. Guidelines
60. Heart Cries
61. Ideas
62. Images
63. Individuals, Groups of People
64. Inquires
65. Insights
66. Injustices
67. Instructions
68. Images
69. Implications
70. Issues
71. Laments
72. Lessons
73. Longings
74. Losses
75. Messages
76. Methods
77. Modes of communication, travels, etc.
78. Misunderstandings
79. Murmurings
80. Needs
81. Observances
82. Observations
83. Operations
84. Opinions
85. Options
86. Patterns
87. Perspectives
88. Phrases
89. Pleas
90. Points
91. Praises
92. Prayers
93. Problems
94. Proclamations
95. Promises
96. Provisions
97. Purposes
98. Qualities
99. Questions
100. Reactions
101. Realizations
102. Reasons
103. Realities
104. Reassurances
105. Recommendations

106. Records
107. Relationships
108. Requests
109. Requirements
110. Remembrances
111. Resources
112. Responses
113. Responsibilities
114. Results
115. Revelations
116. Satisfactions
117. Scenarios
118. Signs
119. Similarities
120. Sins
121. Solutions
122. Specifics
123. Standards
124. Statements
125. Steps
126. Stipulations
127. Strengths
128. Stresses
129. Struggles
130. Successes
131. Suggestions
132. Summations
133. Teachings
134. Temptations
135. Themes
136. Thoughts
137. Topics
138. Transitions
139. Trials
140. Tribulations
141. Troubles
142. Truths
143. Understandings
144. Upsets
145. Voices
146. Wants
147. Warnings
148. Ways
149. Weaknesses
150. Wonders of God
151. Words
152. Works of the Lord

EXAMPLES OF GOOD INTERPRETATION QUESTIONS

In that curriculum writers have often agreed that good interpretation questions are the hardest type of question to write, please study the following questions to glean insights into how to create good interpretation questions. Notice how they are frequently written as follow ups to observation questions. Also review how they answer one of the questions listed under "types of interpretive questions" when endeavoring to interpret a passage. (see page 19).

Examples of Interpretation Questions	Type of Interpretive Questions
1. **Read Psalm 29:3-9.** In what ways is the voice of the Lord described? (O) 2. Considering the descriptions of the Lord's voice in question 1, what do they indicate about hearing and responding to God's voice? (I)	What does this imply? How are these related to each other?
1. **Read 2 Samuel 15:22.** What is God's attitude toward obedience? (O) 2. In light of 1 Samuel 15:22, what might have been the consequences to the eunuch as well as to Philip if Philip had not obeyed the voice of the Lord? (I)	
1. **Read Psalm 131.** In what ways does David describe himself and the present state of his soul? List as many descriptions as you can find. (O) 2. What does David mean by having a stilled and quieted soul within himself? (I)	What does this word or phrase mean?
1. **Read Psalm 51.** This psalm reveals David's burdened plea to God for mercy. Use a Bible dictionary to define mercy. Given the meaning, what must David have realized about his actions? (I) 2. **Verses 1-2** use a Hebrew technique of synoptic parallelism. In these verses, identify three synonyms for unrighteous behavior and three synonyms for pardon. What significance does David's repetition of the same idea have for you, and what might it suggest about David's present emotional and spiritual state?	What does this imply? What is the significance of this?
1. In the NIV Bible, the phrase "Maker of Heaven and Earth" is used five times. Three of those five times are found in the Psalms of Ascent (Psalm 121:2, 124:8 134:3). Why is the use of the phrase "Maker of Heaven and Earth" in Psalm 121:2 particularly reassuring?	Why is this here?
1. **Read Psalm 123:1,2.** The psalmist states in verse, "I lift up my eyes to You, the One enthroned in heaven." What attitudes are reflected by this statement? In verse 2 the psalmist uses two word pictures. Identify the word pictures. (O) What additional attitudes does each one reflect? (I)	What does this imply?
1. **Read Psalm 136:1-26.** For what reasons does the psalmist give thanks? What acts does God perform that give proof of His enduring love? (O) 2. What characteristics of God are revealed through the above acts? (I)	What does this imply?
1. **Read Psalm 137 and Jonah 2.** Record on the following chart the losses that the Israelites and Jonah are grieving and their heart cry to the Lord. Israelites Losses Being Grieved Heart Cry to the Lord (Psalm 137) Jonah (Jonah 2) 2. In contrasting these situations, do you think the Israelites or Jonah were repentant? Why or why not? (I)	How are these related to each other?

HELPING APPLICATION QUESTIONS GET TO THE HEART LEVEL AND NOT STOP WITH THE HEAD

This exercise is to teach you how to make sure application questions get from the head to the heart. Some application questions require FEELING language to help the Bible student make this transition. Unless something hits us on the HEART level, we can easily ignore the question, choose to skip over it and never really apply it. The goal of application is to move our head knowledge down to our heart and out to our feet and hands.

3C. You have just discovered that dire consequences await those who are unsaved. Who, in your own life, needs to be saved? Commit to praying for this person every day during the coming week. Ask God to open the heart of this individual so that he or she will be open to the truth of salvation.

4C. Perhaps the approach you just described is one that you could take the next time an opportunity arises to share your faith and salvation with the person you identified in question 3C. What specific step will you take to prepare for such an opportunity?

4C is a great application question. However, it is written assuming one's heart involvement (on the feeling level) in wanting to take this step.

The follow-up questions below may help get this application from the head level to heart level:

On a scale of 1-10, how would you rate your heart-hunger for seeing those in your life who do not know Christ actually pick up and put on the helmet of salvation?

How can reflecting on the dire consequences that await the unsaved (3C) help to create a deeper heart-hunger in you?

What else might help you *really care* about their salvation?

To apply the principles presented in this exercise, please consider doing the following:

After you have written your lesson, review your application questions asking, "Have I helped the Bible participant move this application from the head to the heart? What feeling words could I use in this question or in a follow-up question that might help with this transition?"

Participles (ing words) Helpful in Creating Day and Lesson Title

1. Abiding
2. Acting
3. Affording
4. Aggravating
5. Ascending
6. Attributing
7. Believing
8. Bending
9. Bemoaning
10. Breaking
11. Building
12. Calling
13. Captivating
14. Centering
15. Changing
16. Checking
17. Comforting
18. Committing
19. Confronting
20. Convincing
21. Desiring
22. Crying
23. Declaring
24. Deepening
25. Determining
26. Discovering
27. Discipling
28. Dying
29. Encouraging
30. Enduring
31. Enriching
32. Embracing
33. Exciting
34. Experiencing
35. Exploring
36. Facilitating
37. Falling
38. Feeling
39. Focusing
40. Finalizing
41. Forgiving
42. Fulfilling
43. Giving
44. Going
45. Grasping
46. Growing
47. Guiding
48. Healing
49. Helping
50. Hearing
51. Hiding
52. Hoping
53. Increasing
54. Initiating
55. Inspiring
56. Knowing
57. Leading
58. Legalizing
59. Lifting
60. Listening
61. Living
62. Living out
63. Loving
64. Marveling
65. Meditating
66. Moving
67. Networking
68. Participating
69. Pleasing
70. Praising
71. Receiving
72. Redeeming
73. Resting
74. Restoring
75. Reconciling
76. Remembering
77. Risking
78. Sacrificing
79. Satisfying
80. Seeing
81. Seeking
82. Showing
83. Silencing
84. Sitting
85. Shouting
86. Sleeping
87. Springing
88. Standing
89. Surrendering
90. Taking
91. Testifying
92. Thirsting
93. Touching
94. Thrilling
95. Training
96. Transforming
97. Transitioning
98. Trusting
99. Trying
100. Turning
101. Understanding
102. Upholding
103. Walking
104. Washing

*Instructions for **working on emailed document** of your lesson:*

1. Your emailed document has been prepared according to a standard template for Women's Bible Study Curriculum. The font sizes and the types of fonts have all been chosen for you.

2. The margins have been preset at .8 top, bottom, right, left.

3. Please do NOT make changes to the fonts or to the margins. If you do NOT have Lucinda Bright italics on your computer (for lesson and day titles), your computer will automatically default to a different font. Use whatever font to which it defaults. I will make changes when you email me the final document. Do not try to change the font to look like the original hard copy we give to you.

4. If you want to include a chart in your lesson, please type in the directions. DO NOT TRY TO CREATE THE CHART ON YOUR COMPUTER. Do not add text boxes. Feel free to draw the chart for me, letting me know about how much room you want for each column and/row.

5. If you would like to help with formatting YOUR LESSON, please do so ONLY according to Vicki's instructions (included in your packet—entitled WOW Curriculum Formatting Instructions).

6. If you would like to help with formatting YOUR LESSON, please do so ONLY according to Vicki's instructions (included in your packet—entitled WOW Curriculum Formatting Instructions).

7. Please do NOT add clip art. Clip art must be well documented. If you have an idea for clip art, please describe it or send a picture as an example.

8. According to correct protocol, only one space is necessary after every period. Since most of us learned to type with a 2nd space after every period, we will create our whole document with a 2 space format even though it is technically no longer correct.

9. Please DO NOT try to format the numbering. Just hit return and type the next number as this document shows. I will format numbering as part of the final document. Please do NOT do the following. It will NOT be helpful:

    1. Question one. Fjggkb kfmfkobovoofmfkgjmbkk b kfgjgjkkj mfnmfkgkggfmgmmbbmbmbmbmbmbmgvgmfmffmfm

    2. Question two Finddkilsdklsn'cvnn'lkfmnm'smnslkfns vcnvnnvvnvn lklkfns'kfnsdfsldkdfmsdkdf

10. **All curriculum writing participants should receive their document—WRTIERS *AND* HELPERS. Save the document. Make a 2nd copy of the document and save it. Please feel free to enter your changes into your 2nd copy, but keep the original to remind you of where you began.**

Sample Curriculum Formatting Instructions

I. Layout

   A. Title Page

      1. <u>Must</u> contain the following statements:

> All Scripture quotations in this publication are from the HOLY BIBLE, NEW INTERNATIONAL VERSION ® NIV ® Copyright © 1973, 1978, 1984 by International Bible Society. Used by permission. All rights reserved.
>
> Most artwork is provided by Microsoft Office Word Clip Art Images: © 1983-2003 Microsoft Corporation. All rights reserved.
> Used by permission. See Bibliography

      2. We have open permission to quote from the NIV translation as long as we do not quote more than 50% of any single book and as long as the quote does not constitute the major portion of our work. Any exceptions to this must be approved by the International Bible Society. This can be done on-line at www.ibs.org

      3. The majority of the artwork used has come from Microsoft Office Word Clip Art. Microsoft allows us to use their images as long as we post the above statement on the title page and in the bibliography. Two other sites permit use of their artwork as long as they are cited in the bibliography:

> http://clipart.christiansunite.com
>
> http://www.biblepicturegallery.com

      Other artwork can be used only if permission is explicitly stated in their User Agreement.
      Please be aware that the majority of artwork found both on the internet and on most software programs is copyright protected and cannot be used.

      4. Always copied 1-sided

   B. Course Syllabus

      1. Lists writing team members

      2. Lists class dates and corresponding lesson numbers

      3. Always copied 1-sided

   C. Unnumbered Page

      1. Serves as a Lesson Introduction

      2. Text usually comprises about 2/3 of the page, with artwork, etc. comprising the remaining 1/3

      3. Always copied 1-sided

D. Lesson Text
1. Morning Study: 8 pages; Evening Study 6 pages
2. Divided into 5 days
3. Each day contains several questions. Multiple questions addressing a specific topic are numbered as a group: for example, 1A, 1B, 1C., etc. Question 2 would indicate a new topic or new flow of thought.
4. Digging Deeper questions
   - Typically 2-3 per lesson or equivalent to 2 pages
   - A soft border and italicized text identifies these questions
   - Always used the Digging Deeper icon:

5. Study Notes
   - Identified in the lesson by a specific font (described below under Fonts)

   - Study Notes are inserted at the end of the study. All Study Notes sources must be documented as used in the Study Notes section. All sources must also be cited in the Bibliography.

6. Scripture References - Scripture references are noted by bold text

7. Lesson Ending
Every lesson ends in the same way: with a recurrent clip-art image of a couple or female jogger.

8. Copied 2-sided, with page 1 always beginning on the right (top) side

E. Repeat C and D above for each lesson

F. Study Notes
1. Numbered sequentially throughout the study
2. Sources are always listed with each quote/reference
3. Copied 2-sided

G. Bibliography
1. Follows standard Bibliography format
2. Copied 2-sided

H. On-going Charts
1. Any charts to be used in more than one lesson are inserted at the end of the study. In the corresponding text, a note stating this is inserted.
2. Copied 1-sided unless multiple copies of the chart are required

I. Header and Footer
1. Header always includes Title of the Study
2. Footer always includes the following copyright statement, as well as the lesson number and page numbers. Each lesson always begins with page 1. Use different pagination for different sections. (For example, number the Study pages with I, ii, iii. etc., the Bibliography with I, II, III, etc.)
Copyright © 200_ by Grace Baptist Church/WOW—Hudson, MA

II. Fonts

    A. Titles

        1. Set apart the titles with a font different than the text. Times New Roman and Palatino Linotype photocopy the best for this purpose.

        2. Title Page: Size 36 pt., italicized

        3. Unnumbered Page Titles: Size 16 pt., italicized

        4. Lesson Titles: Size 16 pt., italicized

        5. Scripture Sections included as part of Lesson Titles: 14 pt., italicized

        6. Daily Titles: 14 pt., italicized

        7. Scripture Sections included as part of Daily Titles: 11 pt., italicized

        8. Study Note and Bibliography Titles: Size 16 pt., italicized

    B. Lesson Text
       Arial, 11 pt.

    C. Scripture Quotations
       Arial, 10 pt.

    D. Scripture References
       Arial, 11 pt., bold
    E. Study Note References

    F. Header and Footer

III. Spacing

    A. Margins .8" on all sides

    B. In text, only one space after each period

    C. Indent Scripture references

    D. Plenty of white space for responses

Lesson Plan Curriculum Writing Team Day 3
Date _____

Time Schedule	Agenda	Page #	Summary of Homework to be completed by late May ___
9:15-9:25	Worship What fresh insight have you gleaned this month from working on your lesson?		Writers edit exchanged lesson with check list in preparation for turning in final draft on May _____ .
9:25 - 9:40	• **Benefits of a Curriculum Writing Team** • **Thinking/Feeling Flow** (PULL OUT AND PUT IN BACK OF MANUAL) • **Instructions for your Introduction** (unnumbered page) (PULL OUT AND PUT IN BACK OF MANUAL)	70 71 73	
9:40 -11:15	• **Review 1st draft** of 2 lessons in groups of 4 (If odd number of lessons, there will be one group of 6/3 lessons) • **Receive** feedback		
11:15 - 11:30	**Regather** as whole group **Share** blessings from today's experience **Review** template with how to edit **Final questions and prayer**		

72

BENEFITS OF TRAINING A CURRICULUM WRITING TEAM

1. **A team brings their collective experience to the writing process**, both biblically and experientially.

2. **The workload can be divided among team members.** No one individual carries too heavy a workload, bears the burden of criticism or even the temptation toward self-glory. Each team member can write a lesson and edit one or two other lessons.

3. After lessons have been assigned and written, to complete the task **team members could function in their areas of giftedness.** Some may be good at layout while others great at editing. Some may shine in the writing of introductions or in the rewriting of excellent application questions. Others may be great at publicizing the start of the new study or prefer to help train the small group leaders.

4. **Team members will grow in depth in their study of God's Word and their desire to teach it to others.** They will also grow in their confidence in handling the Word of God accurately without having to get a seminary degree!

5. **The workbook can be created with the correct number of lessons, the right amount of homework, and the best balance of thinking versus feeling questions.**

6. **The topic or biblical passages can be the primary focus in choosing what will be studied for the year, not finding a workbook that has all the correct criteria for good workbooks,** regardless of the topic or biblical book being studied. Good workbooks geared to the target groups' needs are really hard to find.

7. **The bonding of the team is incredible.** There is nothing more satisfying than creating something for the Lord and His people that has long-lasting impact.

8. **The team concept can be reproduced in other churches if team members are called to a new city or a new church.**

9. **The longer a Bible Study exists, the more difficult it is to find good curriculum,** because the best on the market has already been used in prior years. A curriculum writing team can eliminate or cut down on the endless search for excellent Bible study curriculum.

10. Since most published curriculum are required to have little or no homework, **it is particularly difficult to find good curriculum that requires homework,** if that is the goal of your target group. A team can create curriculum with the desired amount of homework.

11. **A team approach will protect from burnout for an individual curriculum writer.** When burnout or moving away occurs, the Bible study is left wanting. If a team of writers is in place, new team members can be added yearly to replace

Charting the Thinking—Feeling Flow for Lesson _____

Type of Question	1A	1B	1C	1D	1E	1F	1G
Thinking Observation Interpretation S/Cult. Coor.							
Feeling Application Reflective Correlation Warm-up							
Type of Question	2A	2B	2C	2D	2E	2F	2G
Thinking Observation Interpretation S/Cult. Coor.							
Feeling Application Reflective Correlation Warm-up							
Type of Question	3A	3B	3C	3D	3E	3F	3G
Thinking Observation Interpretation S/Cult. Coor.							
Feeling Application Reflective Correlation Warm-up							
Type of Question	4A	4B	4C	4D	4E	4F	4G
Thinking Observation Interpretation S/Cult. Coor.							
Feeling Application Reflective Correlation Warm-up							
Type of Question	5A	5B	5C	5D	5E	5F	5G
Thinking Observation Interpretation S/Cult. Coor.							
Feeling Application Reflective Correlation Warm-up							

74

Instructions for your Introduction (Unnumbered Page)

The goal of the unnumbered page is to introduce the topic of your lesson in a captivating and interesting manner. It should aim to draw the Bible study participant into the feeling aspect of your lesson before asking her to fully engage her mind in a more diligent study of the Word.

Possibilities for top 2/3 of page	Possibilities for bottom 1/3	Possible Sources for Both
1. Short story or historical biography or story about someone's life and how their experience relates to your lesson. 2. Extended analogy or metaphor and how it relates to your lesson. 3. A poem and how it relates to your lesson. 4. A quote and/or expanded principle and how it relates to your lesson. 5. The words to a hymn that ties in closely with the theme of your lesson, giving explanation of the tie in. 6. Please include a transitional statement of how it relates to the lesson. Please don't assume your reader will understand the connection. Please state it clearly.	1. Picture related to your lesson. Most introductory pages will include a picture. (Please feel free to pass on picture suggestions from legal websites to the editing team.) 2. Short quote related to your lesson without explanation. 3. Short verse of hymn or a chorus related to your lesson. 4. Short poem or portion of a poem related to your lesson.	1. Book on history of hymns 2. Internet research 3. Devotional books 4. Bible study workbook introductions adapted from other sources. 5. Christian magazine articles, Christian radio illustrations and sermons. 6. Interviews with missionaries 7. Conversations with friends. Biographies you have read.

Lesson Plan Curriculum Writing Team Day 4
Date _____

Time Schedule	Agenda	Summary of Homework to be completed by late June
9:15-9:25 a.m.	Worship What fresh insight have you gleaned **this** month from working on your lesson?	Final draft of lesson due completed by writer, incorporating suggestions from CW team members. Bring 2 hard copies to class Please email one copy to each member of the editing team **prior** to class
9:25-9:40 a.m.	• Review of **Feedback Process** (page 76) • Request sharing of T-F Flow • Questions?	(Check during class that all emailed copies have been received)
9:40-9:50 a.m.	Work in pairs in preparation for giving feedback	
9:50-11:30 a.m.	• Meet in small groups to give feedback on lessons • Most small groups will consist of one writer/helper team paired with a 2nd writer/helper team. • If your workbook contains an uneven number of lessons, one small group will consist of 3 writer/helper teams.	
11:30-11:45 a.m.	Final questions and concerns	

Preparation for Feedback

1. Review the Concept of Learning Curves
Where you started
Where you are now – be realistic and don't expect perfection!
Receiving feedback is part of your learning curve
You cannot improve without receiving feedback.

> TODAY AND OUR FINAL SESSION ARE IMPORTANT DAYS FOR YOUR LEARNING
> CURVE. THIS PROCESS IS NOT JUST ABOUT TURNING OUT A GREAT FINAL
> PRODUCT BUT TO AID YOU IN YOUR LEARNING CURVE BECAUSE YOUR GROWTH
> AND DEVELOPMENT ARE IMPORTANT TO GOD AND TO US. 2 Corinthians 3:18

2. Review of Process for Receiving and Giving Feedback
Give Positives First
Suggestions Second
As you give feedback, please keep in mind the Forest for the Trees
Concept, trying to help your teammates understand their own trends.
For instance does she tend to see the forest well (the big picture), but miss
the details? Or vice versa? . . .

a. This is what *you* do well
- Great day titles
- Wonderful open-ended observation questions with several answers that will promote discussion
- Your flow of the lesson is clear and easy to follow.
- Great balance of thinking and feeling questions.
- This lesson really made me think! I had to dig to get answers but in a way that was very refreshing.
- Your Scriptural correlation questions show lots of thought and insight.

b. This is the street you seem to keep walking down.
   This is the hole you keep falling into.
- Interpretation questions are not easy for you
- Your reflective questions and application questions (feeling questions) are written like a thinker. We tweaked them in the following way. It was a bit more difficult to really feel as we went through the lesson.
- You need some easy transitional statements.
- We suggest a study note in the following place.

What you do well . . .	The holes you keep falling into

Lesson Plan Curriculum Writing Team Day 5

Date _____

Time Schedule	Agenda	NO HOMEWORK!!
9:15-9:25 a.m.	Biblical reflections that have been stirring your soul	NO ASSIGNMENT! YOU'VE MADE IT TO THE FINISH LINE! CONGRATULATIONS! THANK YOU FOR ALL YOUR HARD WORK! I AM PROUD OF EACH OF YOU!!!!!!!! GOD HAS USED YOU FOR HIS GLORY!

9:20-9:35 a.m.	Review principles of learning curves (page 78)
	    • Personal learning curve
	
	    • Curriculum writing team learning curve (take-aways for next year)	

9:35-9:45 a.m.	Work alone reviewing principles from Preparation for Feedback (page 76)	

9:45-11:30 a.m.	Team shares to whole:
	• Progress on own Personal Learning Curve
	    • what you did well
	    • where you need to improve
	    • how you progressed since last year
	
	• Curriculum Writing Team Learning Curve
	    • where we did well
	    • where we improved over last year
	    • where we could do it better next year	

11:30 a.m.	Final prayers and praise for God's hand upon us!	

LEARNING CURVES

THE LEARNING CURVE EFFECT

The learning curve effect states that the more times a task has been performed, the less time will be required on each subsequent iteration.

THE EXPERIENCE CURVE EFFECT

The experience curve effect is broader in scope than the learning curve effect encompassing far more than just labor time. It states that the more often a task is performed the lower will be the cost of doing it. The task can be the production of any good or service.

What are the implications of the above effects?

Where are you on your learning curve?

What experience are you bringing to the process?

- o Life experience
- o Previous Bible study experience
- o Previous leadership experience
- o Previous Bible study leadership experience

If you choose to be on the curriculum writing team, how will next year's process be different for you because of what you learned this year?

Team Learning Curve
What parts of the team process did you most appreciate? What did we do this year that you want to make sure we will do again next year?

How did the team improve over last year?

What suggestions do you have for how we could do things differently next year?

Would you personally like face-time to debrief after final editing?

YES   (   )

NO   (   )

Name: _____

Made in the USA
Columbia, SC
19 July 2019